PORTRAIT OF MY INNER CHILD

Juliana Cameron

WARNING

This book contains adult language and scenes, including flashbacks of child physical and sexual abuse, which may cause trigger reactions. This story is meant only for adults as defined by the laws of the country where you made your purchase. Store your books and e-books carefully where they cannot be accessed by younger readers.

DISCLAIMER

Names, characters, businesses, places, events, locales, and incidents are either the product of the author's imagination or used in a fictitious manner. Any resemblance to actual persons, living or dead, or actual events is purely coincidental. However, I would classify this book as self-development, rather than fiction.

Although the author has made every effort to ensure that the information in this book was correct at press time and while this publication is designed to provide accurate information in regard to the subject matter covered, the author assumes no responsibility for errors, inaccuracies, omissions, or any other inconsistencies herein and hereby disclaim any liability to any party for any loss, damage, or disruption caused by errors or omissions, whether such errors or omissions result from negligence, accident, or any other cause.

This publication is meant as a source of valuable information for the reader. However, it is not meant as a substitute for direct expert assistance. If such level of assistance is required, then the services of a competent professional should be sought.

For more information or any enquiries visit: BondiNanny.com

"*Let's raise children who don't have to recover from their childhood.*"

~ Pam Leo

*"In the little world in which children have their existence,
whosoever brings them up, there is nothing so finely
perceived and so finely felt as injustice."*

~ Charles Dickens, *Great Expectations*

Dedication

I dedicate this book to all survivors of childhood abuse.

Acknowledgement

To my dear friend Steve who has been like a father figure to me—a Capricorn man, a stable and secure ship who was there for me when I felt lost and overwhelmed in stormy seas. Thank you for believing in my dreams and for believing in this book.

CONTENTS

INTRODUCTION: A NOTE FROM GYPSY

"You're a Child of the Universe, no less than the trees and the stars!"

~ Max Ehrmann, *Desiderata*

If you had the chance to have a conversation with your younger self, what would you say? What lessons and words of wisdom would you share?

I'm passionate about both learning and teaching, my motivation for studying education.

I should start by introducing myself. Gypsy is my nickname, yet it feels like my authentic name. The name was born out of a fragmented upbringing where I led the life of a Gypsy— pulled in and out of many different homes, many different schools, in many different suburbs, in many different cities and different states; passed around to friends, relatives, foster homes by a mother too invested in her man to care for a child.

I'm a survivor of childhood abuse and domestic violence. Some say there is still a stigma with being a survivor. Perpetrators always seem to have at least some protectors and enablers. Some people call them Flying Monkeys. Protecting the perpetrator is still a priority for some people in our society, either because they're a doormat or an abuser themselves.

I believe some adults want to forget what it was like being a child. Why? Because being a child ultimately meant being vulnerable. Sometimes it meant being controlled or restricted to various degrees. Growing up I wondered, *When was I going to be allowed to participate in life?*

As I penned my way out in a journal, I've had to visit very dark places, places that as the "quiet child" I had rarely expressed. Yet I felt driven to do so.

In the movie *Rocky,* one particular scene resonated with me loud and clear. In it, Rocky Balboa (Sylvester Stallone) says, "Let me tell you something you already know. The world ain't all sunshine and rainbows. It's a very mean and nasty place and I don't care how tough you are, it will beat you to your knees and keep you there permanently if you let it. You, me, or nobody is gonna hit as hard as life. But it ain't about how hard you hit. It's about how hard you can get hit and keep moving forward; how much you can take and keep moving forward. That's how winning is done!"

Though child abuse is shocking and takes great courage to look back on it, I felt compelled to speak up and speak out against my abusers, no matter how overwhelming and painful it was at times.

"There is no coming to consciousness without pain," said Carl Jung.

And what a cathartic journey it has been, helping me evolve more into my true being. This book is the book I would have given to my teenage self to help me re-parent.

Pain travels through generations until someone is ready to heal it by making a positive change. We must protect children's eyes and ears, for what they see and hear can leave an imprint on their minds and hearts for a lifetime. Whenever I see a baby or child staring at me, I always smile at them. I want them to feel like their little world is safe, friendly and caring.

"The most beautiful people we have known are those who have known defeat, known suffering, known struggle, known loss, and have found their way out of the depths. These persons have an appreciation, a sensitivity, and an understanding of life that fills them with compassion, gentleness, and deep loving concern. Beautiful people do not just happen."

~ Dr Elisabeth Kübler-Ross, *Death: The Final Stage of Growth*

Sharing my story will help to address the myths and misconceptions that some non-survivors have about childhood abuse, especially in relation to victim-blaming attitudes.

Although I welcome anyone to read this journal and share my journey, I've written this book primarily for other survivors who I hope will see it as educational and raising awareness, but of course not a replacement for professional help. If you too had insensitive and abusive parents, you don't have to accept the messages from childhood. My exploration into the darkness will hopefully inspire you to explore yours as well.

Sharing stories is cathartic. "It is liberating and healing to hear the stories of other survivors," wrote Debra Wright. "Their bravery is astounding, and their validation is what makes it easier to move forward. I cannot thank them enough because they truly get it."

"Knowledge is **power**. *Information is **liberating**. **Education** is the premise of progress, in every society, in every family."*

~ Kofi Annan

When we educate ourselves through learning about someone else's life, we feel empowered to go on with our own lives, while engaging empathy for others. I say "go on" with our lives and not "get over," as you may never "get over" a stolen childhood. We learn to live with recovering and repairing becomes Art.

Kintsugi is a Japanese art form in which breaks and repairs are treated as part of the object's history. Broken ceramics are carefully mended by artisans with a lacquer resin mixed with powdered gold, silver or platinum. The repairs are visible — yet somehow beautiful. Kintsugi means "golden joinery" in Japanese.[i]

Another reason to hear stories of other survivors is because child abuse is often shrouded in secrecy. You may have thought something *off* about your stepfather or mother or mother's boyfriend(s), something that being so young you wouldn't have been able to understand. Even women in adult relationships report feeling disorientated by abuse. Imagine how overwhelming this must be for a child to comprehend. I was overexposed and underprepared.

My parents always tried to tell me I was "too sensitive."

Not wanting to parent me, my "mother" and "stepfather" didn't care about my wellbeing and welfare, or me. As an unloved and unwanted daughter, I received messages like "You don't matter," "Your feelings don't matter," "You're worthless," "You're not important," "You're a drag, a chore and a burden," and "You're in the way." The list went on, my childhood stolen by abuse—from beatings to denying my basic needs for wellbeing to inappropriate sexual conduct.

By acknowledging the repercussions and ramifications of my childhood through writing I was able to triumph and become an "artist."

I love art and I love education.

"Education is the most powerful weapon we can use to change the world."

~ Nelson Mandela

Educating ourselves provides us with that A-ha moment; it empowers us. We need to make sense of the senseless, a need to sort through and organise the confusion and trauma. We need to clean up the crazy chaos, to put it to rest and let go. Only then will it no longer continue to haunt us.

I remember Brené Brown once said, "Only when we are brave enough to explore the darkness will we discover the infinite power of our light."

To heal, survivors need to write their stories, to tell their stories and share their stories in whichever outlet they feel safe. We are all healers in the world if we choose to use our gifts. Gloria Steinem once said, "Recognizing this compelling self of the past can help to keep us from repeating history. Otherwise, we may continue to treat ourselves as that child was once treated."

For years, I engaged the young minds of children from early childhood to primary. Now, I wish to work with adult minds to inspire you to interact with your inner child.

With my preschool children, I would provide educational activities to teach them about sorting and patterns. Sorting is classified as a beginner math skill. Yet from personal experience I know it's a great skill in general.

Children have a natural desire to make sense of their world. As adults, it's important we retain this desire, to make sense of our world.

My understanding and insights come from my own survival experiences, as well as many years of research and reading on the topic of childhood abuse and narcissism.

My story is my gift to you, for you to begin or to continue your own journey deep within. Hopefully, this will also help you to change how you treat the child within. I hope the exploration of my own childhood inspires you to explore yours too.

I've included a poem below from "anonymous" that resonates with me. It portrays how much we can gain from learning about the personal experiences of others. Learning from the experience of other survivors gives us a hand up so we can break free of the addiction—the addiction of thinking that the drug or the abuser is good when they are actually toxic.

"Do not underestimate the power of a child's desire to believe his or her mother is a good person—even when the child is being abused."

~ Seymour Epstein, *Constructive Thinking: The key to Emotional Intelligence*

Before we have broken free of an addiction or an abuser, we may feel confused and disorientated; we may also feel like an addict.

An addict fell into a hole and couldn't get out. A businessman went by. The addict called out for help. The businessman threw her some money and told her to buy a ladder. But the addict could not find a ladder in this hole she was in. A doctor walked by. The addict said, "Help, I can't get out." The doctor gave her some drugs and said, "Take this, it will relieve the pain." The addict said, "Thanks." But when the pills ran out, she was still in the hole.

A renowned psychiatrist rode by and heard the addict's cries for help. He stopped and said, "How did you get in there? Were you born there? Did your parents put you there? Tell me about yourself; it will alleviate your sense of loneliness." So, the addict talked with him for an hour, then the psychiatrist had to leave, but he said he'd be back next week. The addict thanked him, but she was still in her hole.

A priest came by and heard the addict calling for help. The priest gave her a bible and said, "I'll pray for you." The Priest got down on his knees and prayed for the addict, then left. The addict was very grateful, and she read the whole bible, but she was still stuck in that hole.

A recovering addict happened to be passing by. The addict cried out, "Hey, help me, I'm stuck in this hole." Right away, the recovered addict jumped in the hole with her. The addict said, "What are you doing? Now we're both stuck here." But the recovered addict said, "It's okay, I've been here before, I know the way out."

JOURNAL ENTRY 1 – A WAY OUT

"There is no greater agony than bearing an untold story inside of you."

~ Maya Angelou

A writer writes because she has something personal to share.

When people ask me, "Where are you from?", I feel lost in how to reply—"home" was an elusive concept. A place isn't what makes a home, it's animals and people. "Home is not a place, but rather, the people you love," said writer Jodi Picoult.

For me, "home" was a horror chamber of abuses, a place where I felt scared, alone, neglected, left out and unloved.

I've read books about Marilyn Monroe, who spent many years in foster homes where she was allegedly sexually abused. Like her, I was abused, severely neglected, and abandoned to foster homes and, like her, I wondered how to find a Way Out.

What would be my way out from the trauma of my childhood? I believe the way out is to GET IT OUT.

For me, it proved to be through writing. I learned that sometimes you have to go back to move on. Keeping it all in isn't brave. Feeling the pain and facing it takes courage.

And so, I wrote my journal as a way to find my voice, to use my voice and have my voice heard, after suffering a childhood where I was silenced. Each journal entry was like an artistic representation of and created by my inner child; a portrait.

Some say to never keep a journal. Because someone else might find it, and God forbid, read it. Yet here I am, writing this as if you will find it and read it. I must. Writing empowers me and serves as a catharsis and I've been passionate about writing since a child.

Left alone much of the time when I was young, writing was always there for me. To play ball or a game, someone has to spend time with you. To write, you need only yourself. Nor did I have to seek permission from anyone to write.

And writing helped me to connect with others, like my schoolteachers, and authors of books that greatly influenced me. For instance, books by Roseanne Hawke, an award-winning Australian author from Penola, South Australia who has written over 25 books for young adults and children, and who teaches tertiary-level Creative Writing at Tabor Adelaide; and books by John Marsden, an Australian writer and school principal who began writing books for children when he worked as a teacher. I eventually met them both through writing workshops and festivals, via one of the primary schools I was enrolled in.

Another way out has been a passion for learning and self-development and I've done much research and reading. It's why I'm an avid collector of quotes; they're like Pearls of Wisdom.

I'm an artist and I've always been an artist. I love the word 'Artist' because it encompasses everything I love to do, including acting, dancing, writing, drawing, photography and education.

"Teaching is a calling too. And I've always thought that teachers in their way are holy—angels leading their flocks out of the darkness."

~ Jeanette Walls

The more knowledgeable we are, the better we will be as families, a community and society.

When we use our personal experiences to help others, our life experiences are transcended into a gift. In this way, we learn from each other, using our different strengths. Heaven on earth exists when we help each other.

"Experience is the hardest kind of teacher; it gives the test first and the lesson afterward."

~ Oscar Wilde

As a renaissance woman, I'm at my happiest when I'm creating art or admiring art. This journal has been one of my many artistic passions, both a creative and cathartic outlet for me. "I will write myself into wellbeing," said Nancy Mairs.

This journal is like my collage, a personal art portfolio filled with clippings of my favourite quotes, research, personal journal entries, vignettes, poems—whatever resonates with me.

Sometimes writing is better than talking. Often when you talk, people don't hold space for you: they interrupt; they dismiss; they give "advice." Take my friend Roy. When I shared with him that I believe people's childhoods have an impact, he said, "It's gone, everybody's childhood is gone. It's over."

Yet our childhoods are not water under the bridge. To heal and recover from childhood scars, we have to acknowledge the repercussions and ramifications of our early years. Recovery starts with recognition because understanding ourselves depends on first understanding our childhood.

We need to clean up the crazy chaos, to put it to rest and let go. When we help ourselves to let go, our childhood doesn't continue to haunt us. Have you ever come home to a messy room and feel that you can't rest or relax until you organise it? Well, we have to do the same for ourselves, for our wellbeing and welfare.

When I started my studies in Early Childhood Education and Care and first read the Early Years Learning Framework, I burst into tears. Supporting the Early Years Learning Framework is the perspective that children's lives are characterised by Belonging, Being and Becoming. One of the principles is secure, respectful and reciprocal relationships. When children feel safe, secure and supported, they develop confidence and a strong identity. As an unloved and unwanted daughter, I know from personal experience how our childhoods create a ripple effect.

Almost seventy years ago, psychologist Abraham Maslow devised a hierarchy of everyone's basic needs.

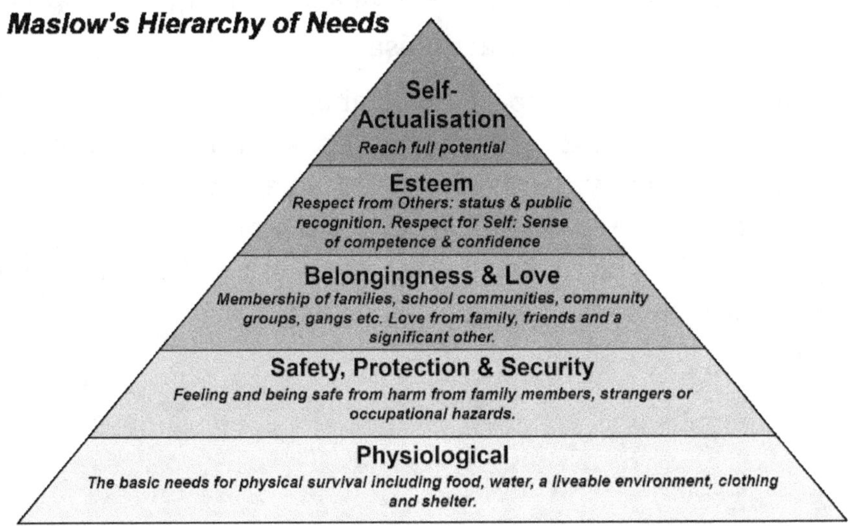

Barely feeding me, not caring how well I slept, or if I had the proper clothes to protect me from the weather, my mother and stepfather neglected my physical health, depriving me of the first need for survival: basic physiological needs. Perhaps they had hoped I might die because they resented my very existence.

Beating me, shaking me, pushing me, sexually abusing me and abandoning me, my mother and stepfather made me live in fear for my life, depriving me of the second need: security and safety from harm.

Criticizing me, demeaning me, ignoring me, they violated the third basic need: love, family and a sense of connection.

Not having valued or appreciated me, not caring about my schooling—sometimes not even enrolling me in school as we moved from place to place—they violated my fourth basic need: to feel competent and confident (self-esteem).

All this abuse and neglect made the last, the need for self-actualisation impossible. Only when I became an adult and worked hard and long to play catch up on the first four basic needs of which I had been deprived could I begin to develop my own identity and self-actualisation.

Research warns that experiencing abuse and neglect in childhood can lead to adverse outcomes in adulthood; that women who were victimised as children are at risk of re-victimisation as adults. This has been my personal experience. Maybe that's why as a woman I seem to attract so many unreliable and transient type people.

Yet I've survived it all.

JOURNAL ENTRY 2 – ALL THE ABUSE: HOME OR HELL?

Tonight, I thought back on some of my earliest childhood memories from when I was growing up in Adelaide, Australia.

The youngest of four daughters, I was born to a single mother in her 40's. Misha, the oldest daughter had moved away to live on campus to study teaching when I was born. Our Mother had bought a small three-bedroom trust home in Adelaide that the rest of us all lived in together. Mum lived in one of the bedrooms and her second eldest daughter, Anne, had one of the other bedrooms all to herself. The daughter Lynne, the "golden child" and my Mother's favourite, and I shared the remaining bedroom.

As a child, I suffered all five forms of child maltreatment:

- Physical abuse.

- Sexual abuse.

- Emotional abuse.

- Psychological abuse.

- Child neglect.

Physical Abuse

Physical abuse is the second most common form of child maltreatment. It occurs when a child is severely and/or persistently hurt or injured by an adult or a child's caregiver. It may also be the result of putting a child at risk of being injured.[ii]

Some examples are:

- hitting, shaking, punching

- excessive physical punishment or discipline.

Possible signs of physical abuse are:

- broken bones or unexplained bruises, burns, welts

- the child is unable to explain an injury, or the explanation is vague

- dehydration

- the child is unusually frightened of a parent or caregiver

- arms and legs are covered by clothing in warm weather

- brain damage through shaking or hitting.

Sexual Abuse

The World Health Organization (WHO) defines child sexual abuse (CSA) as "the involvement of a child in sexual activity that he or she does not fully comprehend and is unable to give informed consent to, or for which the child is not developmentally prepared, or else that violate the laws or social taboos of society."

The term CSA includes a range of activities like "intercourse, attempted intercourse, oral-genital contact, fondling of genitals directly or through clothing, exhibitionism or exposing children to adult sexual activity or pornography, and the use of the child for prostitution or pornography."

Sexual abuse can take many forms, including physical and non-physical behaviours.

Physical Behaviours

- Touching a child's genitals for sexual pleasure or other unnecessary reasons.

- Forcing a child to touch someone else's genitals.
- Putting objects or body parts inside the vulva or vagina, in the mouth or the anus of a child for sexual pleasure or other unnecessary reasons.

Non-physical Behaviours

- Exposing a child to pornography.
- Encouraging a child to perform sexual acts.
- Exposing a person's genitals to a child.
- Performing sexual acts in a child's presence.
- Photographing a child in sexual poses.
- Watching a child undress or use the bathroom, often without the child's knowledge.
- Using computers, cell phones or social media outlets to make sexual overtures or expose a child.[iii]

Emotional/Psychological Abuse

Emotional abuse occurs when an adult harms a child's development by repeatedly treating and speaking to a child in ways that damage the child's ability to feel and express their feelings.[iv]

Some examples are:

- constantly putting a child down
- humiliating or shaming a child
- not showing love, support or guidance
- continually ignoring or rejecting the child
- exposing the child to family and domestic violence
- threatening abuse or bullying a child

- threats to harm loved ones, property or pets.

Possible signs of emotional abuse include when a child:

- is very shy, fearful or afraid of doing something wrong

- displays extremes of behaviour; for example, from being very aggressive to very passive

- is not able to feel joy or happiness

- is often anxious or distressed

- feels worthless about life and themselves

- has delayed emotional development.

Child Neglect

Neglect is the most common form of child maltreatment. According to WHO (2006, p.10) neglect includes both isolated incidents, as well as a pattern of failure over time on the part of a parent or other family member to provide for the development and wellbeing of the child—where the parent is in a position to do so—in one or more of the following areas:

- health

- education

- emotional development

- nutrition

- shelter and safe living conditions.

Within that home, I was also exposed to domestic violence.

JOURNAL ENTRY 3 – STRANGER DANGER: MUM'S NEW BOYFRIENDS

Desperate to not be alone, Mum would bring men home the first night she met them, and they came and went like a revolving door. Two of them, Melvin and Quirky, were abusive intruders who compromised my safety. I had to fight them off constantly.

My Mum didn't care. "I have to have a life of my own. I can't be a mother," she would tell me.

When I was around four, I was in the bathtub and Melvin barged into the bathroom. I wrapped my arms around my body, terrified. I screamed, "MUM! MUUMM!" Smirking, he put his finger up to his mouth in a "Shh" motion and stepped closer to the bathtub.

My mother didn't come in. But he left the bathroom because I kept calling out for her.

Did he touch me while I was in the bathtub? No. Did he sexually molest me? No. Was I still sexually abused? Yes. I was exploited. In hindsight, it was clear that he was "perving" on me. He invaded my right to privacy. He also wanted to look at my little naked body for his own gratification, even when I clearly communicated my distress. He violated me and that is a form of childhood sexual abuse. He gained gratification in feeding his own sexual addiction, not just by looking at women but little girls too.

Info Point: "Many other non-touching behaviours, such as routinely 'walking in' on children while they are dressing or using the bathroom, can be inappropriate and harmful even though they may not be illegal. It is important both for the sake of the child and for the person who is acting harmfully or inappropriately that adults intervene to protect the child and prevent the person from committing a crime."[v]

Article 16 of the UN Convention on the Rights of the Child (UNCRC) states that children have the right to privacy.

After that bathtub incident, I remember fighting off Melvin yet again. While watching television, I heard yelling. I scurried cautiously into the kitchen. Melvin was smashing everything— cups, glasses, dishes. I cowered quietly in the corner.

He grabbed a knife and pointed it at my mother's throat.

I flew to her side. "Don't hurt Mummy!"

"You stupid brat," he screeched and chased after me around the house, knife still in hand.

Catching me by the hair, he dragged me into my bedroom. He shut the door and locked it and pushed me onto the bed.

"MUMMY! MUMMY!" I screamed. I struggled to pull away from him and make my way back to the door to escape but I couldn't.

Dark! He turned the light off. "MUMMY!" I yelled in the direction of the door.

Why wasn't my Mother helping me? Why wasn't she at the door screaming? Where was she? I struggled to break from his grip.

"You slut!" he said, the smell of liquor burning my eyes.

Red Flag: Men linking sex and aggression together by using the word "slut" is a warning sign. Research has shown men will yell out verbal violence like the word "slut" before a physical act of violence.

He turned the light on and whacked me across the face with his hand. The blow knocked me down and I cowered, my hands covering my head, my body shaking, my hands sweating, my heart pounding.

"MMUUMMYY!" I screamed as he tugged at my clothes to pull them off. I tried to crawl away from him towards the door.

Finally, I heard movement on the other side. Someone was trying to get the door open. "UNLOCK THE DOOR, IT'S THE POLICE!" I collapsed into tears. Someone was here to save me.

My sister Anne had heard Melvin and Mum arguing earlier and called the police because she knew Melvin had been beating mum.

Mum didn't hug me when she saw that I was ok. She yelled, "Now you've ruined everything! He'll never come over again. It's your fault, you little brat."

The next day I looked in the mirror of the little dressing table that I shared with my sister Lynne. Staring back at me was the reflection of a little girl with a man's handprint plastered on the side of my face in red. Later, I realised that hand mark was a sign that I had saved my mother's life. If I hadn't walked into the kitchen and ran to her side when he pulled the knife on her, what would have happened? Would he have stabbed her to death before the police came?

Witnessing domestic violence, another form of child maltreatment, continued throughout my childhood. When my mother later married Quirky, my stepfather, they would have the worst fights.

Caregiver Tip:

Don't allow random boyfriends/stepfathers in the bathroom while your child is bathing or changing. Your child has the right to privacy. Do not allow random men to be left alone in charge of "caring" for your child. Any man that wants to meet a mother's child should be expected by law to have a Working with Children Check clearance number. Also, spend time getting to know a man before you bring him home to your child/children.

JOURNAL ENTRY 4 – LOST CHILD

On one rare occasion, my oldest sister Misha visited me and brought me a black and white panda bear teddy. I was thrilled and grateful. Nobody had ever given me a teddy bear before. It was so nice to have a moment where I could be a child, especially after Mum's boyfriend had hit me and called me a slut.

After a few hours, Misha stood up to leave.

"Where are you going?" I asked.

"I have to leave to go back to uni." My older sisters Anne and Lynne hugged Misha goodbye before she walked out the door and I followed her.

"Don't go, please don't go," I said.

"I have to, I live on campus."

"I wanna come with you."

"I can't bring you with me. Go back inside." I was so sad as I watched her walk away. I felt we had a rapport.

I chased after her down the road.

She turned around.

"I don't wanna go back inside! I don't wanna go back home!" I said, sobbing.

She walked me back to the house. Anne and Lynne kept me locked inside the house while Misha left. I watched from the window as Misha walked away, tears rolling down my face.

Red Flag of Child Abuse: Not wanting to go back home.

JOURNAL ENTRY 5 – DON'T TELL YOUR MOTHER, GOD IS WATCHING YOU!

I remember lying on the floor. Quirky is shaking me violently. My mother had gone to work and left me alone in the house with this boyfriend whom she barely knew, something she did often.

Everything is spinning which he seems to take pleasure from. Laughing, he tells me he's fond of shaking because "Shaking leaves no bruises or marks on the face, but it will make your head spin."

Disorientated, I close my eyes and pull my legs into the fetal tuck. He had shaken me so hard my shoulders and neck ached for days. He wanted to shatter my sense of safety and security with neglect and physical abuse before the sexual abuse started.

"Don't tell your mother about this," he says while kicking me in the back, my side, my butt, apparently having changed his mind about leaving no marks. "GOD IS WATCHING YOU," he says. At four years old, God is taken literally. The thought that God might be watching me guaranteed that I would keep my mouth shut. Eventually, he stopped saying "Don't tell your Mum about this" when he realised that my own mother never cared about me.

Finally, he storms out of my bedroom, as if it's he who had something to be angry about!

Quirky physically abused me. Even worse he emotionally abused me. He had terrified me, which studies show to be as damaging, if not more so than physical abuse.

In hindsight, I realise everything he was saying was an admittance of his own guilt. He knew what he was doing was wrong and yet still chose to do it. It wasn't a loss of control but a choice.

Later on, I learned that he was quite capable of remaining cool and calm when faced with men who were bigger and stronger than him. Yet he didn't show the same restraint with women and children because he was a coward.

Info Point:

Cinderella Effect: In evolutionary psychology, the Cinderella Effect is the phenomenon of a higher incidence of different forms of child abuse and mistreatment by stepparents, than by biological parents.

JOURNAL ENTRY 6 – MUM'S NEW "MAN" IS THE MOST DANGEROUS MAN IN A CHILD'S LIFE

A real man doesn't victimise a child. After many short-term, often one-night boyfriends, good old desperate single Mum constantly brought home my biggest childhood nightmare: Quirky. Three months after she met him, he became my stepfather.

Before Quirky entered our lives, I had a bit of reprieve from the constant terror and abuse between her one-night stands or when she was out on a date. Now, with Quirky as her husband, my life became one of maltreatment.

Neither Mother nor Stepfather ever wanted to be parents to me and never made me feel a part of the family. Instead of protecting me, they enjoyed hurting me. Quirky perpetrated a litany of abuse upon me, from beatings to denying my basic needs for wellbeing to inappropriate sexual conduct.

I wasn't given good food or even enough food when I was a child. Neglecting me, Mum kept all the good food locked away in her bedroom for herself.

I was always so hungry and Quirky would eat in front of me and refuse to share. He wouldn't even let me eat the leftovers my mother had put aside for me.

One incident, in particular, stands out. My mother had gone to work and left me alone with Quirky.

He was sitting at the kitchen table eating. I hadn't had breakfast and I was hungry.

"I want cereal," I said.

"It's not my job to feed you," he said, not even looking up and continuing to stuff his mouth.

"But I'm hungry."

"You'll survive."

I stared at him, tears rolling down my eyes. Annoyed, he got up from the table, dragged me to my bedroom and shook me until the bedroom was spinning. Then he shoved me to the ground.

I tried to crawl away from him, but he picked me up and shook me again, slammed my back against the door and shoved me back to the ground, adding physical abuse to the neglect of my well-being.

Neither Mum nor my sisters Anne and Lynne were home. Nor were the police there to help me this time. I was on my own.

After this, I knew I could no longer ask him for food as he would only try to hurt me further. He loved to taunt me about being hungry. He enjoyed withholding basic human decency. He enjoyed punishing.

He had planted a poisonous seed: *You can't rely on others to get your basic human needs met.*

JOURNAL ENTRY 7 – PARENTAL SNOBBERY

At the dinner table, Quirky didn't let me share anything about my day at school. If I tried to participate in the conversation, he would tell me that I'm not allowed to. If I tried to talk to my mother about her day, she would turn to Quirky and say, "She thinks she knows what we're talking about."

Quirky would make snide comments about the way I looked. He would say, "You're so skinny, if you turned sideways, you'd disappear!"

He knew that I was being sent to school with no lunch. He knew that he was leaving me at Anne's place, after she had eventually moved into her own place, in a dark room with no food. He knew that I was only being given tiny amounts of leftovers for dinners. Yet here he was making snide comments about how skinny I was. As a woman, it's no wonder I ended up having a yo-yo relationship with food.

Once I dared ask, "Why do you and Mum get all the special food and I don't?"

"IF YOU'RE REALLY THAT HUNGRY, YOU'LL EAT IT!" he screamed at me. I would quickly wolf down whatever they were willing to give me for dinner after having spent the school day starving. When I asked, "May I be excused?" Quirky would stare at me and say, "Yes. JUST GO!"

Maybe all that parental snobbery as a child turned me into a workaholic as a woman.

JOURNAL ENTRY 8 – HUNGRY AT SCHOOL

I always felt hungry at school because my parents sent me without lunch. I would watch my mother make a variety of different sandwiches for Quirky, along with a container of fruit salad and a container of cheeses and olives.

"Why don't you ever make a sandwich for me too?" I asked.

She looked at me, stunned. "Why would I bother making anything for you? Besides, you probably wouldn't eat it anyway."

She gave me cereal for breakfast and dinner. For recess and lunch at school, I always went hungry while I watched the other children eat. Later, when I worked at early education centres, I felt like crying with happiness when I saw how much effort parents put into making their children's lunches.

I was sent to school not only without lunch, but without a hug or kiss on the cheek, or well wishes of "Have a great day." Watching the other children being kissed and hugged and loved and told, "Have a great day, sweetheart" was missing from my childhood and made me sad.

At home, Mum rarely hugged me, nor did Quirky. He loved pushing me to the ground and kicking me in the back. "No one will see the bruises at school because your back is always covered in clothing," he said and laughed. He thought he was so clever, but really, he was just cunning and deceitful.

JOURNAL ENTRY 9 – ALONE & STARVING

During school holidays and weekends, my mum and Quirky would leave me all day in a darkened room without food or water at my older sister Anne's place.

Anne now had a one-bedroom apartment. At night, she would go out drinking and clubbing. She didn't return home until 6 or 7 am. Then she'd sleep until the late afternoon and keep her bedroom door shut.

Quirky had the spare key to her place because Anne didn't want her sleeping to be disturbed. He'd drop me there at 8 am and pick me up at around 6 pm. When I asked for food, he said always that he didn't have any. When I asked him for some books to read while I was there, he said that he didn't have any. He never even gave me a water bottle. He never opened the window or curtains for me. He just left me there in the darkness all day. He would point and say, "Sit there and stare at the wall."

"Our greatest need and most difficult achievement is to find meaning in our lives."

~ Bruno Bettelheim, *The Uses of Enchantment: The Meaning and Importance of Fairy Tales*

There was no TV in the dark and small lounge area I was left in. Anne had the television in her bedroom. To help her to "wake up" she'd watch TV in bed for a few hours alone in the late afternoon. All day I would look at the ticking clock on the wall and wait for when the big hand was on the 12 and the little hand was on the 4 to hear the TV. Then I knew she was awake.

Sitting alone in the dark lounge room next to her bedroom and listening to the clock tick on was torture. I never knocked on her door as she had always warned me not to. I wasn't wanted by Mum or by her.

I would ask Quirky why I couldn't stay home with mum. He would say, "Because your mum wants the place to herself during the day."

When I asked mum directly, "Why can't I stay home with you?" she would say, "Because I don't want you around. I want the place to myself."

"But I'm hungry in that dark room."

"Well, just ask Anne to make you a piece of toast."

I started crying and shouting, "BUT I ALREADY TOLD YOU, SHE SLEEPS ALL DAY AND HER DOOR IS SHUT!"

"DON'T SPEAK TO YOUR MOTHER LIKE THAT!" my stepfather shouted back.

When my stepfather brought me home in the evening, he and mum would call me a pig when I wolfed down the dinner they gave me. "But I haven't eaten all day. I feel starved."

"Oh well," Mum said. "It's just for the holidays and weekends." Quirky would smirk and snigger, gloating to see my mum didn't care about me.

It was the wonderful world of art that made me feel seen, heard and understood. When I grew up and watched the movie *Great Expectations*, I could relate, especially when Estella shared her humanity with Finn about being a little girl who was taught to fear daylight. One of the most emotive films I've ever watched and every scene featured the colour green, symbolic of growth and evolution.

JOURNAL ENTRY 10 – SHOPLIFTING

Constantly hungry and neglected by Mum and Quirky, I started shoplifting at the tender age of five. When I was with Mum at the grocery, I would run off to the candy aisle and stuff as many chocolates as I could in my pocket. She bought chocolate and bagels for herself, Quirky and for Lynne the Golden Child. But never for me.

I remember always staring at the checkout chick wondering if she knew that I had candy stuffed in my pockets. When we got home, I'd hide the candy under my pillow and my bed. I would try to make it last as long as possible, scared that there was never enough.

Whenever I hear of others shoplifting, I wonder whether they too were starved as a child. Did they never get their basic needs met in childhood either? It took me a while to grow out of the habit.

As a survivor of childhood abuse, I believe it's crucial to learn about abundance. I loved learning from Louise Hay and Wayne Dyer's teachings on abundance.

JOURNAL ENTRY 11 – HOW NARCISSISTS TREAT CHILDREN

"The bond that links your true family is not one of blood, but of respect and joy in each other's life."

~ Richard Bach

Mum and Quirky were pathological narcissists who got off on mutually abusing me as a child. It was like a form of foreplay to them. There was a sickness in their head. It's called *narcissism*.

Narcissism is the experience of feeling important, needing admiration and attention, and wanting success and love.[vi] It's normal and, if mild and occasional, can even be a healthy personality trait. A healthy level of self-interest relates to positive traits such as confidence, resilience, and having dreams and goals that support a growth mindset.

It's another story altogether if you have a narcissistic personality disorder as my mum and stepfather did. Narcissism is the biggest killer of relationships.

Experts warn that narcissism is on the rise which is why I believe in the importance of promoting a unity consciousness.

Narcissistic Personality Disorder (NPD)

When narcissism is extreme, you have a narcissistic personality disorder.

Those with NPD have an inflated sense of importance. Often described as emotional "vampires," narcissists do not feel empathy or compassion and don't connect with others. Possessing a deep need for excessive attention and admiration, they believe the world revolves around them and others serve to accommodate their needs and wants. Self-absorbed, they do whatever pleases them at the expense of others, even at the expense of an innocent child.

Nine key symptoms are associated with NPD. To be diagnosed as having NPD as assessed by a medical professional, you must experience at least five of the following:

- A grandiose sense of self-importance.

- Preoccupation with fantasies of unlimited success, power, brilliance, beauty, or ideal love.

- A belief that they are "special" and unique and can only be understood by, or should associate with, other special or high-status people (or institutions).

- An intense need for excessive admiration.

- A sense of entitlement—that they should get and have whatever they want.

- A tendency to be interpersonally exploitative—that is, they use others to achieve their own ends.

- A lack of empathy demonstrated through an unwillingness to recognise or identify with the feelings and needs of others.

- Envy of others, or the belief that others are envious of them.

- Arrogant, haughty or supercilious behaviour and attitudes.

Quirky was a true narcissist. He believed Mum and I were there just to please and serve him. He had no interest in giving, only taking. The joy of giving evaded him. All attention had to be focused on him. I think he treated me so cruelly because he demanded Mum's attention at all times.

Women can be just as narcissistic as men, but research tells us that more men suffer from it than women. "We love our boys and raise our girls," said Michelle Obama when she raised the subject of whether parents are enabling entitlement in boys.

My Mother was also a somatic narcissist. These are people obsessed about their bodies and sex. Mum chose the "look at me" approach.

One morning, while waiting at the front door in my school uniform to be taken to kindergarten, Mum said, "Quirky, look at this," and opened her dressing gown to reveal her naked body underneath.

I still remember all the lumps of cellulite she had over the front of her legs, and how her legs were covered in varicose veins—blue and purple ripples all over her legs with lumps of cellulite. Everywhere were stretchmarks. Her chest resembled shrivelled tiny prunes. She always complained that giving birth four times made her body look worse.

I was repulsed and still feel repulsed by the ugly vision and memory of her conducting herself like that in front of me.

The hair on her head was black as the big hairy lump of black bush she had between her legs. In hindsight, I now wonder whether it was also as black as her heart—if she had a heart. She was just an ugly person, in general, to conduct herself like that in front of a child.

When my mother exposed herself, Quirky whistled and made salacious noises. I find it obnoxious and intrusive to hear a man wolf-whistling or whistling to a tune from a song.

Whistling of any kind reminds me of my tawdry stepfather
and I just want to escape!

JOURNAL ENTRY 12 – MUM & QUIRKY: JEKYLL & HYDE

Most people know the story of Jekyll & Hyde, where a person displays two opposite personalities: one good, one evil.

The Jekyll side of Mum and Quirky was well-behaved. For example, they would never sexually abuse me in front of their friends or colleagues.

Narcissists, mostly show their nasty Hyde side in private. And this nasty side came out more and more, as typical of narcissists, they devalued me more and more in put-downs, insults, gaslighting, lack of emotional or physical intimacy, withdrawing affection, disappearing, or blaming their target for their own behaviour, also known as projection. Their Jekyll-and-Hyde behaviour made me feel like Alice at a Mad Hatter's Tea Party, though it was much more maddening than that.

Quirky sexually abused Mum in front of me in a free-for-all. They told people in front of me that they wanted to get rid of me. My mother would say, "I've already raised three daughters. I shouldn't have to do it a fourth time with this one," she said as she pointed to me. Quirky chimed in, "She's not my daughter anyway."

Desperate mum even once said to her friends in front of me, "I want to have sex with my husband in front of the fireplace, but we can't because of my daughter. She might come out of her room to go to the bathroom."

They spent thousands of dollars on the yacht plus thousands more in regular maintenance. Then they'd tell me that they can't spare $10 per week on dancing lessons for me. They could only spare thousands on themselves and their dreams with the yacht.

What about my childhood?

They never showed any interest in my passions.

They never cared about who I was as a person.

They were typical textbook narcissists; they both wanted me to give up everything, to be their nothing.

JOURNAL ENTRY 13 – UNRIGHTEOUS DOMINION

I walked into the lounge. "Hiiii," I said in a cheerful voice to Mum and my stepfather, trying as always to establish a good parent-child relationship with them.

Quirky screamed at me, "GO FIND YOUR OWN TREE!" and then started sexualising my mother.

I burst into tears and ran to my bedroom where I collapsed on the floor in front of the window and sobbed uncontrollably. Every day, without fail, they reminded me that I was an unloved and unwanted daughter.

What a horribly hateful man, from the finger he pointed at me to the hateful tone of his voice. I missed Grandma and her cat Jaimie so very much.

When I eventually studied Early Childhood Education and Care, I read about the importance of communicating to children that you are happy to see them. From my personal experience, I couldn't agree more!

Interestingly, Quirky never sexualised my mother when his brother or work colleagues and their wives were over for lunches and dinners on the weekends. In other words, his sexualising in front of me didn't come from a lack of control. It came from a cowardly deliberate abuse of power!

The bible refers to narcissism as an Unrighteous Dominion— an abuse of power. Quirky would even say to his colleagues, "Look at what a great family man I am. I married a single mum who has a daughter from some other man." He would then point to me in contempt.

Domestic violence, bullying and cyberbullying are all epidemics and they all stem from narcissism which means caring about others is more important than ever!

Info Point: "Unrighteous Dominion can involve spiritual, religious, and ecclesiastical abuse and/or a more general abuse of perceived power or authority. It can manifest within marriages, families, or relationships within the church, such as between a bishop and a church member."[vii]

Info Point: Men who choose to give in to their temptation to exercise unrighteous dominion exists in any situation where one is in a position of power or influence. It can occur at school, work, church, your community and in homes and families. A man who practices unrighteous dominion in his home single-handedly destroys the confidence of his wife and children.

Sadly, Quirky never displayed affection to Mum. He never held her hand or kissed her cheek. Disrespecting her, he treated her like a free prostitute.

Info Point: "Displays of affection are a good thing to express in front of children. What is not appropriate: mature sexual language, groping or putting his hands down her pants, and having sex or wanting to have sex or intimate relations with her child/children around. Further, it is sexually abusive, and can be reported to Child Protective Services (CPS)."[viii]

JOURNAL ENTRY 14 – MEANINGFUL RELATIONSHIPS

"Relationships never die a natural death … They are murdered by ego, disrespect, selfishness or disloyalty."

~ Anonymous

Life is about relationships. When we foster meaningful relationships with children, we give them the luxury of learning how to swim, before they reach the deep waters of adulthood. In this way, children develop acceptance and self-esteem necessary for positive learning and life outcomes.

My narcissistic parents did not foster healthy relationships with me.

Fortunately, I would later find warm relationships with my teachers when my parents bothered to send me to school.

While the relationship between caregivers and children is first and foremost as that's where it all starts, it takes a village to raise a child as the saying goes. Each relationship has a ripple effect. For this reason, relationships are important not just with parents but within our schools and communities.

National Quality Standard

Child Australia recognises the importance of a shared understanding of high-quality pedagogy in its early childhood education and care services.[ix]

Though these standards are designed for teachers and caregivers in a school setting, they apply as well to what should be the gold standard for parents.

The importance of developing relationships with children is reflected under "Quality Area 5 of the National Quality Standard."[x] This is reproduced below.

Standard 5.1: Respectful and equitable relationships are developed and maintained with each child.

Rarely was I ever treated respectfully by my parents or sisters, only when I was with my grandmother I felt respected.

Element 5.1.2: Each child is able to engage with educators in meaningful, open interactions that support the acquisition of skills for life and learning.

"Good relationships early in life help children to connect with others, build positive friendships and support children to self-regulate their emotions. For relationships to be meaningful, interactions need to be warm, caring and responsive."[xi]

A great educator and a great parent are an emotional anchor for a child. An emotional anchor is reliable, trustworthy, nurturing and present. This provides a child with stability and security to give them the confidence to face the world to interact, learn, explore and grow.

Mum and Quirky used an anchor for their boat but never for me. That rope connecting the anchor to the yacht and you to your child is like an umbilical cord, channeling security and stability. Though my mother and stepfather were supposed to be my emotional centre, my secure base, they never held out an emotional anchor for me. No wonder I felt like a lost little girl.

Element 5.2: Each child is supported to build and maintain sensitive and responsive relationships with other children and adults.[xii]

I never received this support as this memory demonstrates.

My mother came back to the car with a sandwich to eat. While she was eating, I pointed to the playground that we were parked next to.

"Come play with me over there," I said.

"No," she replied, "You can go by yourself."

I looked out the window again and saw a man at the playground. I didn't feel safe.

"No. There's a man there. Come with me."

She refused and said she just wants to eat her sandwich and then drive home to get ready for one of the social dances. This was before she had met my stepfather, Quirky. Meeting men was her priority and she couldn't even spare ten minutes to be an emotional anchor for me at the playground.

"When attention is given to building connections and maintaining them over time, children are more likely to feel a sense of security, wellbeing and belonging. To build positive relationships with others, children need to develop 'social competence' and the ability to interact with others with care, empathy and respect. Social competence is the foundation that allows children to understand and self-regulate their own emotions and negotiate their interactions with others."[xiii]

Only by interacting with other children can a child build social competence. This, my mother, denied me over and over by keeping me alone during much of my childhood.

Because of this, I didn't know how to relate to other children. I would sit alone in the playground and watch the other children laughing, playing and running around, carefree.

Element 5.2.2: Each child is supported to manage their own behaviour, respond appropriately to the behaviour of others and communicate effectively to resolve conflicts.[xiv]

Neither my mother nor my stepfather ever taught me to communicate effectively. Disrespected, demeaned, ignored and neglected, I remained quiet to not anger them and further invite their anger and often violence. My only form of communication was to try and remain invisible.

Similar to these elements were other important guidelines I found as an early childhood teacher: The Early Years Learning Framework (EYLF) and the 'My Time, Our Place: Framework for School Age Care' both of which share the same five outcomes of:

1. Children have a strong sense of identity.

2. Children are connected with and contribute to their world.

3. Children have a strong sense of well-being.

4. Children are confident and involved learners.

5. Children are effective communicators.

The frameworks also share five principles:

1. Secure and respectful relationships.

2. Partnerships.

3. High expectations and equity.

4. Respect for diversity.

5. Ongoing learning and reflective practice.

As a survivor of child abuse, I know the importance of caring. Neither my uncaring mother nor stepfather could ever steal my capacity to care which I gave lovingly to the children I taught according to the above guidelines.

You don't have to accept the messages from uncaring, unloving parents.

Running the before- and after-school childcare department at one of the School of the Sacred Heart colleges was one of the highlights of my career. Danielle, the principal was a beautiful person. I could feel the magic resonate from her during assemblies when she spoke on stage about the importance of teaching children about resilience. Working there as the Lead Educator and Coordinator of my department was very meaningful for me.

Jack Ma, the founder of Alibaba, believes in the importance of meaningful relationships too. After watching a video of him speaking at a press conference, he said that only by changing education can our children compete with machines. (Robots could replace 800 million jobs by 2030.) "We have to teach something unique so that a machine can never catch up with us. These are the soft skills we need to be teaching our children. Values, believing, independent thinking, teamwork, care for others."

Exercise:

Write a list of the qualities that you like about yourself. Examples may include caring, responsible, thoughtful, sweet and considerate.

Write an example of something you did that demonstrated each quality you have. For example, if you write "Showing Initiative" you could then list all the courses, studies and self-development you've done. It's like a gratitude list, yet it's directly about you.

Write a nightly gratitude list before you go to bed. This will help you show up for your inner child by making that child seen and heard in a positive light.

Caregiver Tip:

Write out a list of all the amazing qualities about your child. Or leave a little note in their lunchbox wishing them a wonderful day.

These kinds of gestures make children feel seen and loved. When I worked as a live-in nanny, I would place cute little notes in the children's lunchboxes. I would write, "Have a great day at school/kindy today. Mummy loves you, Daddy loves you, and I love you too."

I would also add that the family pet loves them too and draw little paw prints. When I picked the children up from school, they would bring up the note and laugh and smile about how cute it was. One of my younger children, who was still at kindy, smiled and said the teacher read out the note for him and said it was lovely. These small acts of kindness make big differences in a child's world.

JOURNAL ENTRY 15 – RE-PARENTING

"When I became a man I put away childish things, including the fear of childishness and the desire to be very grown up."

~ C.S. Lewis

It's crucial to make time for the fun and play that we were never allowed to have as a child.

When I watch documentaries about the miracle of childbirth and new life, I feel pangs of sadness for the love I never received. I was repeatedly forced to take the blame for being a "burden." My stepfather Quirky would often grab me by the arm and say, "Apologise to your mother for being a burden. Say sorry to your mother for being born. Tell your Mother you're sorry for being alive."

Eventually, after many years, I reached a point where I no longer cried when being instructed to say sorry for my existence. Yet I am crying while writing about this because this journal is giving me a safe space to grieve.

Through self-love, we can re-parent and give ourselves the meaningful relationship we never had. This is what I'm doing for myself with this journal. Before I started writing it, I had not properly grieved for my inner child and was always in survival mode. Now I allow myself time and space. This includes walking away and taking a break when writing becomes overwhelming.

By committing to caring for ourselves, we enhance self-love. The more we foster a meaningful relationship with ourselves, the more able are we to attract more reliable people into our lives. And the more we will show up for others in a meaningful way.

As I write in my journal, I hear the sound of crickets outside my home. I've always loved that sound and have always found comfort in nature.

As a little girl, I loved watching David Attenborough's documentaries. Though my stepfather never allowed me to be a little girl, I felt I could relax and be one while I watched David Attenborough talk about the beauty of nature and animals. Intrigued, I felt a sense of wonder and awe.

Survivor Tips/Exercises:

What we attract in our adult relationships may be similar to what we experienced in our childhood. If we suffered child maltreatment, we would carry that pain into adulthood.

If there was no reliable and emotionally safe caregiver to provide you with a meaningful relationship, you too may struggle to provide this for yourself as an adult. Your life may feel like an emotional desert. To heal you must show up for yourself by becoming conscious, mindful.

If you had a difficult childhood, you don't have to accept the messages from your early childhood. To break a habit, you need to replace it with another habit.

Here are some helpful ways to re-parent.

Repeat Affirmations: I replaced the pattern of messages from early childhood with affirmations by the beautiful Louise Hay. For example, "I am worthy of love," from *You Can Heal Your Life*. Repeating these affirmations in front of the mirror is especially powerful.

Identify What Ways You Neglect Yourself: How long have you been telling yourself that tomorrow will be the day you start working out? Or tomorrow will be the day that you eat more fruit and veggies and less sugar? Or tomorrow you'll stop smoking? Or tomorrow you'll start educating yourself with more reading and less television?

Put pen to paper and list all the ways that you can make a commitment to yourself, to start showing up for yourself. For example:

- Schedule in that morning walk.

- Schedule in regular reading time.

- Schedule in time for fun and play, like your favourite hobby.

Self-care: Eat well, exercise and sleep soundly. By taking good care of ourselves we give ourselves the care and love we never received as a child.

Self-nurture: Do things to help you look forward more than back. Make a list and schedule in your diary, things like getting your nails done, buying a new book, doing a new course, a hobby, cuddling and patting cats and dogs! After all the cruelty we endured as children, we need to provide ourselves with plenty to look forward to as adults.

Pay-it-forward: Doing good deeds for others is a wonderful way to feel the joy of giving.

JOURNAL ENTRY 16 – IT'S ALL ABOUT HIM

Once my mother married Quirky, family decisions rested on what Quirky the narcissist wanted. Though he earned a good income as a radiographer in a permanent position, he kept on wanting to move. They didn't care that I had to play catch up with my education and with my life. It was all about Mum and Quirky's needs. The chaos was overwhelming.

At first, he wished to move to a different suburb in Adelaide. Then he wanted to move to Gladstone. Then Cairns. Then he wanted to do radiography locum work (providing cover for a position left temporarily vacant) in Rockhampton and other places too. Then he wanted to go overseas. Then he wanted to move to Brisbane to be closer to his brother. At another time he announced that he wanted to spend eight months sailing along the Australian coast. And then he wanted to do a road trip around Australia.

Every time the two announced we were moving again I would burst into tears knowing again I would have to play catch-up. My childhood was one big crazy merry-go-round all centred around Mum and Quirky. The eczema on my neck, the inside elbow of the forearm and behind the knees acted up and I would be constantly scratching.

"STOP SCRATCHING your eczema. You're making it bleed!" yelled my poor excuse of a mother.

"I can't! It itches."

"Ignore it," she would say.

How could my mother let this man come into our lives and let him do this to us? How could she be so disloyal to her own daughter? Her own flesh and blood?

I would especially start scratching my eczema when Quirky would sexualise my mum in front of me.

Info Point: When we experience a stressful situation, the body goes into fight-or-flight mode and responds by increasing the production of stress hormones like adrenaline and cortisol. When the body produces too much cortisol, it can suppress the immune system and cause an inflammatory response in the skin. Stress and Anxiety are common triggers for Eczema.[xv]

"Stop scratching your eczema, you look ugly," my mother told me.

Funny how she didn't care about the core of the problem: Quirky's inappropriate sexual behaviour in front of me. They were the ones who were the real picture of ugliness, with the inappropriate way they carried on in front of a child. They were just pigs in mud.

Often, when we moved to a new place, Mum and Quirky would keep me out of school, sometimes for months at a time because we were going to move again soon. Even though keeping a child out of school is illegal in Australia, Quirky still did it anyway, as if he and Mum were a law unto themselves. Metaphorically, they kept pulling the rug out from under my feet.

When they did put me in school, some schools put me down a year level because I was so far behind in my education. It was humiliating and devastating to feel so excluded and so far behind. Some of the schools I remember included Hackham, Aldgate, Sterling, Bridgewater, Mylor, Rockhampton, Cairns, Ashgrove and Kelvin Grove.

I would work hard to be placed back in my correct year level. Then Quirky would pull me out of school again. If I dared complain, Mum would try to justify it. "We won't bother putting you in any school for a few months as we'll be moving again soon."

"When a flower doesn't bloom, you fix the environment in which it grows, not the flower."

~ Alexander Den Heijer

Sometimes they dumped me at my grandmother's house. Grandma's home was a male-free environment, my safe place, my sanctuary. When I was there, my eczema would disappear because the anxiety and stress disappeared. And so, I stopped self-harming.

I would show Grandma and her cat Jaimie my arms and neck and say, "Look, the eczema went away!"

"You've blossomed!" Grandma would say.

Unfortunately, the eczema would always come back whenever I was back around Mum and Quirky.

JOURNAL ENTRY 17 – NEGLECT

Some of the motels we stayed in when we moved had three rooms: one bedroom, a bathroom and an adjoining kitchenette/lounge area with a couch that had a fold-out bed. Other motels just had one bedroom with a kitchenette in the same room and a separate room for the bathroom.

In those motels, Mum and Quirky would sleep in the one bed and shut me away in the bathroom where I slept on the cold, tiled flooring. I was always catching a chill and feeling run down. They would get down on me for this, oblivious to their abuse having caused my constant sickness.

I had to resort to much effort to boost my immune system after everything I endured as a child. I take vitamins daily, drink lots of pure water, and exercise to give myself the consistent self-care that I never received as a child.

JOURNAL ENTRY 18 – RUNNING ON EMPTY

One morning in primary school, we were about to go down to the oval and run a race. I asked the teacher if I could use the bathroom.

"You'd better go now, and you can meet us down at the oval. We'll wait for you before we start the race," he said as I'd told him I didn't want to miss out on the race.

It's so uncomfortable running when you need to pee. So, after I relieved myself, I ran down to the oval to find that he had started the class race without me. He lied. He was just another man that I couldn't trust.

"Heeyyyyy! You started the race without me!" I called out, he turned around and said, "Oh well, you'll just have to try and catch up."

"Go! My teacher kept yelling, "JUST GO, try and catch up!"

That seemed to be the theme of my childhood—trying to catch up to all the other children who had been given a head start over me.

Sighing, I ran past him and looked ahead at all the other children in front of me. I used them as my focus point while running. Even though the other children looked so far in front, I had to keep running. I had to keep moving!

My legs were shaking, and my back was in pain. But I was determined to catch up. Determined! I've always been determined! I believe I was born that way, with the grit gene (an actual gene that makes you persevere).

It was one more instance of having to catch up. Successful people have always fascinated me. Success is subjective—everyone has a different definition of success. I've always wanted to be successful, yet I felt so consumed with just trying to survive.

When I grew up, I watched an amazing educational video about privilege. After my own personal experiences, to say that it resonated with me is an understatement. The narrator announced to the contestants in the race, "I'm going to make some statements. If those statements apply to you, I want you to take two steps forward. If those statements don't apply to you, I want you to stay where you are."

- Take two steps forward if both of your parents are still together.

- Take two steps forward if you grew up with a father figure in the home.

- Take two steps forward if you never had to worry about where your next meal was coming from.

In summary, the narrator explained that some people have a head start in life. Some people will have a better chance of winning this race called life. Regardless, we all have to run our race: ON YOUR MARKS, GET SET, GO!

For a survivor like myself to be successful, I was going to have to be more relentless than life itself.

JOURNAL ENTRY 19 – BEING AN EMPATH

I've always been an Empath. I have a great capacity to care, to feel compassion, to listen to and to connect with others, and to be sensitive to suffering in the world. This was the reason for my activism work, which I'll talk about later, and for being a vegan. As a child, adults would comment on how good-natured I was.

My narcissistic "parents" preyed on my affable and sweet nature. As big babies consumed with getting ONLY their needs and wants fulfilled, they were insensitive and dismissive of my needs and wants. They wanted attention to revolve ONLY around themselves and were dangerous to my development.

I tried so hard to teach them how to love, how to care, how to listen, how to understand, how to empathise. But narcissists are incapable of such feelings.

Emotional vampires like the narcissist gain supply from your pain. There's nothing you could do as a child or an adult to "fix" the narcissistic parent because your hurt and unhappiness are what feeds the narcissistic abuser. Your pain makes them feel superior. The narcissist will never see you as a child, friend or partner, or anything but a form of narcissistic supply.

If you too suffer greatly because of narcissists in your life, here are some things you can do.

Survivor Exercises:

Become Aware of Repeated Patterns

Identify from the nine key symptoms associated with NPD as listed in Journal Entry 11 any traits that remind you of people you know, people who display similarities to the abusive adults in your childhood.

It is important to be aware of the people and patterns we attract in our adult lives and whether they represent the people and patterns that were present in our childhood. We start to recognise the blueprint that we received from the family dynamics of our early childhood. Recovery starts with recognition.

Take Acting Lessons!

Yes, that's right, you read it correctly! Acting lessons can be very therapeutic! As a child you were probably made to feel like it was never safe to come out of your shell. Acting lessons with an emotionally safe and professional acting coach will help you to break free.

Improvisation and role-playing will help you practice having a voice and verbalising thoughts, wants, needs and demands, even if it's via a script! It will help you to overcome vulnerability and provide you with the practice of "putting yourself out there" again. Every time I took drama classes in high school, many of my classmates would say, "Gypsy, you've finally come out of your shell!"

Caregiver Tips:

Ask Questions

Children are naturally egocentric. Don't take what they say personally. Ask open-ended questions if a child says something that is concerning.

A child once repeated an aggressive comment in class. I asked, "Where did you first hear what you just said?"

He replied, "I heard it on the cartoons."

Play-acting

Acting games like Charades can be loads of fun with you and your child/children.

JOURNAL ENTRY 20 – THE NEW GIRL

Every time we moved and I was placed in a new school, I was the "New Girl."

How painful it was to listen to the other children's conversations about how their parents took them to the ocean on the weekends when I would be stuck in a dark room, or about how their mother had bought them new school clothes when my mother didn't care and only gave me hand-me-downs, or about how their grandmother baked them yummy chocolate chip cookies when I very rarely saw mine.

I was an outsider, not belonging with other children. Even if I wanted to make the effort and sidle next to someone who looked kind at lunchtime it wasn't worth it. In no time, I would have to say goodbye again.

So, I spent my lunch breaks in the school library reading, alone. That was how I survived.

"Solitary trees, if they grow at all, grow strong," said Winston Churchill.

Luckily, learning came easy to me because I got little to no help at home. Once I asked Quirky to help me with my math homework. He snarled and said that he was busy and called me every name under the sun. I never asked him for help again.

As for Mum, she was always too busy making sure all of Quirky's needs were met to help me with anything.

Info Point: Australian Prime Minister Scott Morrison said that schooling and education for children are important. For this reason, there should be a maximum number on the number of schools a child can be pulled in and out of. And there should be welfare check-ups on children who have been pulled in and out of too many different schools, and children who have been absent from schooling for months at a time.

JOURNAL ENTRY 21 – ABANDONED

Having been beaten and neglected by Quirky (sexual abuse would soon be added to the list) I now suffered yet another blow to my safety and wellbeing: abandonment.

After their wedding, Mum and Quirky went on a long honeymoon holiday and Lynne and I stayed at Grandma's house. I loved my grandmother and her cat Jaimie. Grandma was a lovely person and such a lady. She would always wear dresses and an apron. Unlike Mum and Quirky, she was calm and patient. Mum was always so highly strung and stroppy, while Quirky would swing from pedantic and pompous to exploding with rage.

When they returned, Lynne and I moved back in with our mother and new stepfather. Soon, my mum announced that I wasn't a "good fit" for the family. She was going to try and arrange foster care for me so she could live just with her golden child Lynne and her husband Quirky. Throughout my childhood, mum dumped me with other people whenever she could. Many times, she threatened to send me to boarding school.

"I thought we were going to be a family? I was your flower girl!" I said between sobs.

"You should be happy for ME!" Mum screamed. "My wedding was about me, not you. You're not part of the family."

I fled to my room in tears.

Why Narcissistic Parents Devalue and Discard Us

Narcissists become demanding and angry, bitter or unaware that other people have their own needs and a separate self. A narcissistic parent will devalue and discard you no matter what you do. They may devalue and discard you over an act that they perceive as a threat to their ego, or a failure to act. This is because a narcissist is unable to emotionally attach to anyone in a healthy way, regardless of whether you are a child or an adult.

You did NOTHING wrong as a child. Please remember that!

On the Outside, Looking In: Sent to a Foster Home

I was soon in a foster home, feeling abandoned, alone, scared and homesick for a home I never really had. Many months at a time they dumped me in many different official and unofficial foster homes. On one of these occasions, they spent almost a year sailing around the Australian coast and I never got to see my mother.

Info Point: Psychiatrist Dr W. Hugh Missildine offers an "Index of Suspicion" for an adult with a neglected child within:

If you have difficulty in feeling close to others and "belonging" to a group or drift in and out of relationships casually because people do not seem to mean much to you, or if you feel you lack an identity of your own, suffer intensely from anxiety and loneliness and yet keep people at a distance, you should suspect neglect as the trouble-making pathogenic factor in your childhood. An additional clue suggesting neglect: prolonged separation from your parents, particularly your mother, by death, divorce, hospitalisation or because of parental activities and interests.

In some ways being there seemed better—at least at first. The daughter, Barbara, the daughter of one of my foster parents, was around the same age as me. We sat on the floor together playing with her dolls and felt happy. My mother never gave me any dolls or toys as a child. She would only buy things for Lynne, the Golden Child.

Barbara's mother was as cruel as mine was. She would tell me, "Your Mother never calls to ask about you. YOUR MOTHER DOESN'T CARE ABOUT YOU!"

One day, her mother walked into the room when we were laughing and playing with the dolls. She screamed at me, "NO! You're not allowed to play with any of her dolls! They're my daughter's toys, not yours!"

The mother grabbed the doll from me and put it in the big box of dolls. "You're only allowed to watch my daughter play with her toys. You're not allowed to join in!"

After grabbing the doll from me, she dragged me into a corner of the room and hit me. I tried to cover my face with my hands to stop the blows. My body cringes when I recall my little body huddled in the corner of the room shaking with terror.

Again, I was excluded. Not belonging anywhere. Not good enough to be anything to anybody. Unworthy. Rejected. Forgotten. Unsafe. Left out, on the outside, looking in.

When was I going to be allowed to participate in life?

Fortunately, or perhaps not so fortunately, the woman complained to my parents that she found it hard to take care of another child and my parent reluctantly took me back in.

JOURNAL ENTRY 22 – EARLY CHILDHOOD MESSAGES & ECHOLOCATION

"Emotional security, community, a sense of being loved unconditionally for oneself—all those turn out to be as important to a child's development as all but the most basic food and shelter."

~ Gloria Steinem, *Marilyn*

In 1963, the year after Marilyn Monroe's death, Dr W. Hugh Missildine published *Your Inner Child of the Past.* Based on his observations, he wrote an analysis of adult emotional problems based on his nine years as director of the Children's Mental Health Center in Columbus, Ohio.

He believed the child we used to be lives on inside us. It is difficult to change those early patterns because they feel like "home."

The only way to change is to recognise the pain of our inner child.

I've always had an affinity with animals. My furry friends gave me the unconditional love my narcissistic parents never gave me. Being a Piscean Mermaid, I've also always felt a connection to my ocean friends too. Reading about and discovering Tilikum the whale was of great help in helping me recognise the pain of my inner child.

Tilikum, nicknamed Tilly, was a captive orca who spent most of his life performing at SeaWorld Orlando. It is unnatural for whales and dolphins and other animals to be kept in captivity. They're meant to be wild and free in the ocean. The confinements of his captivity were similar to the confinements of my childhood and I cried a flood of tears.

Tilikum was locked away at times with no interaction and treated as a commodity, just like I was as a child. He suffered bullying by other captive whales, and stress from being separated from his wild family. His plight was similar to how my stepfather bullied me and separated me from my mother who colluded with him.

The only good that came out of the whale's captivity was a changing perspective. As *Blackfish* co-writer Tim Zimmermann recently wrote for National Geographic, "His life has changed how we view Sea World and the marine park industry and changed our moral calculus regarding the confinement and display of intelligent, free-ranging species."

Like the whale, dolphins too are captured and kept in captivity. I first saw a captured dolphin as a child. Through the hospital he worked at, Quirky and his colleagues were all given tickets to Sea World in Australia. Sea World stole the right of whales and dolphins to remain in the ocean, their natural habitat.

Mum and Quirky sat me down on one of the jetties. They told me that they'd be back later when the show starts and then they left to get something to eat, excluding and starving me as always. In my 20's and involved with activism, I learned that dolphins at Sea World are kept hungry in captivity.

I felt someone staring at me, someone's energy burning into me. I turned around to see a dolphin looking at me, swimming up to the side of the jetty, to be closer to me. It was awe-inspiring to have that magical moment with the dolphin. He started talking to me. I held out my hand and he nuzzled it. I touched him so gently on his body and was amazed at how soft his skin was.

Then we both just stared at each other and spent time together on the side of the jetty. Maybe that Dolphin recognised that I too was in captivity.

"Dolphins are the Einsteins of the Animal World," someone once said.

I learnt about sonar, also referred to as echolocation, and how it provides toothed whales, including dolphins with the gift of hearing and detecting things with precision for hunting, navigating and communicating. Baleen whales—for example, humpbacks and blue whales—generally produce a series of sounds, termed "songs", used for communicating. A whale will send out its sounds and songs and the sound waves will reflect off a fish swimming toward the whale. The whale will use those reflected sound waves to determine where the fish is and in what direction the fish is swimming.[xvi]

Captivity creates stress for the dolphins in many ways. According to an article on CNN, *Captured Dolphins Aren't Smiling*, by Fisher Stevens, "They [dolphins] hate to be enclosed in their holding tanks and are often not fed until it is time to perform their daily routines ... they would get depressed, stressed out, even suicidal. In some parks, the trainers have to give the animals Maalox and Tagamet to treat the ulcers that develop from their stress."

Just like the eczema that appeared on my skin from stress with the captivity of my childhood, dolphins also suffer from this too in captivity.

"Photos obtained by The Dodo from a visitor to SeaWorld Orlando's Dolphin Cove show lesions on the animals' skin that appear to be the result of poxvirus, a disease that can be induced by the stress of captivity. Naomi Rose, a marine mammal scientist with the Animal Welfare Institute, confirmed that the lesions appear to be evidence of poxvirus. We also spoke to Heather Rally, a marine mammal veterinarian with the Oceanic Preservation Society, who agreed."[xvii,xviii]

Because I so identify with the captivity of whales and dolphins, I greatly appreciate the work of Ric O'Barry, an American activist who has been protecting dolphins since the 1970s through the Dolphin Project.

Just like these animals need to be wild and free to use echolocation to navigate the ocean, children need positive early childhood messages to navigate the world.

JOURNAL ENTRY 23 – SCAPEGOAT

Throughout my childhood, Mum would say, "I can't wait to get rid of you. When I get rid of you, I'll finally be able to get on with my life."

What was ironic was that she was getting on with her life and at my sacrifice. I sacrificed my education for her by being pulled in and out of so many schools. I sacrificed a parental relationship with her when she dumped me in foster homes. I sacrificed my childhood, which she had stolen from me. Yet, she always insisted on scapegoating me anyway.

Scapegoating is the practice of singling out a person or group for unmerited blame and consequent negative treatment. That was me. While Misha and Anne were old enough to be independent and Lynne was the Golden Child, I was the youngest and an easy target for all the blame.

It was hard to accept that I couldn't rely on my own mother for love or even protection. All I wanted was to escape the pain of not being wanted, loved and a meaningful member of the family.

Living alone as an adult gives me peace of mind, a sense of control over myself and my space.

Info Point: "Both male and female survivors may have difficulty in trusting and allowing emotional closeness or intimacy. This may also lead to a conscious decision to never have children of their own." (NAPAC)

JOURNAL ENTRY 24 – LOOKING FOR A WAY OUT

How could I escape my childhood hell? There must be a way. One night I dreamt of a beautiful white horse with wings. The horse was in a tower with me, next to an open window.

"Please take me away from here," I pleaded to the horse.

"It's not your time to leave yet," he replied. "I have to prepare you. Your mother is going to betray you. I'm visiting you to warn you. When she does, the best thing you can do is close your eyes, think of a pleasant place and go there inside your head. This will help you survive until you're old enough to escape."

The horse then flew away. I chased after him, but he'd gone before I could reach him. I froze in terror. I tried moving my arms, but I couldn't move my body. I couldn't run, I couldn't even walk. I called out to the white horse, "Please come back. Please don't leave me here. Please."

I woke up sobbing.

This precognitive dream foretold of the horror that was coming.

JOURNAL ENTRY 25 – GROOMING: A GATEWAY

"In fact, most childhood sexual abuse does not involve intercourse."

~ Beverly Engel

Sometimes, paedophiles will buy gifts for a child and be charming and build trust to groom them. That's not what happened in my survival story. It's not always the stereotype of the stranger offering sweets. My stepfather "groomed" me by talking sex and sexualising my mother in front of me, before eventually sexually assaulting me directly.

My "stepfather" was just a sexual predator and my "mother"—well, all she cared about was the trouser snake. Both were inappropriately sexual in front of me. Often, my childhood felt like being held hostage in a nightmarish pornographic film I wasn't even old enough to consent to.

I feel like I've divulged too much too soon. Yet, there never seems to be a good time to share something so traumatic, which is why survivors are so brave in sharing their stories.

Info Point: "Most often child sexual abuse is a gradual process and not a single event. By learning the early warning signs and how to effectively step in and speak up, sexual abuse can be stopped before it starts and a child is harmed. Adults must take the primary responsibility for preventing child sexual abuse by addressing any concerning or questionable behaviour which may pose a risk to a child's safety."[xix]

JOURNAL ENTRY 26 – STOLEN CHILDHOOD: TALKING SEX

I was five years old and smiling for all the group photos that the photographer had asked me to be in for my mother's marriage to Quirky. Suzy, one of Quirky's biological daughters stared at me with hatred. "Instead of saying 'Cheese' for the photos, say 'SEX'!" she screamed at me. I looked at her confused. What did she mean? I didn't even know what "sex" meant.

Frightened, I turned and looked at my mother who ignored me.

Again, Suzy repeated, "Just SAY SEX."

I looked at Quirky, my soon-to-be stepfather. Laughing, he repeated, "Just say sex!"

I felt so alone, small, powerless, and frightened. The wedding wasn't a celebration for me. It was a harbinger of the hell my life would become.

I understand, in hindsight, that she was angry to see her father remarry decades after divorcing her real mother. But at age five all I could feel was hurt and confused.

Quirky continued to make inappropriate sexual comments. One time he said in front of me, "We should start f—— in front of your daughter." I will never forget my mother's evil laugh when he made appalling comments like that.

Another time he said, "You'd be surprised about how sexually experienced your mother is. I could tell you. I could share with you what she knows."

I said nothing. I was so scared. I was so sick and tired of all the stress. Being harassed, threatened, abused, and disrespected was too big a burden for a child to bear.

He showed disrespect in so many ways. One time when I was in the shower, I heard knocking on the door, "Let me in," Quirky said. "I need to get something out of the bathroom."

I got out of the shower, put my clothes back on and unlocked the door.

"Oh, you didn't need to put your clothes back on!" he said.

In the car alone with him, he would talk sex on the way to school. If a romantic song was on the radio, he'd put a sexual twist on it and ask me, "Do you think that man wants to take her pants off, the woman he's singing about?" He would also talk about how he could be my first sexual experience.

I would say nothing and clutch my school bag close to my legs and chest as if using it as a shield to protect my body from him. When I would get to my classroom, I would look so shaken the teacher would often ask, "Are you okay? You look so upset."

Info Point: "If you suspect child sexual abuse, trust your gut. You may be the only one who can take action. Children don't have the knowledge or language skills to be able to know or identify or communicate sexual abuse.

Studies show that in as many as 9 out of 10 cases, children don't tell anyone when they are being sexually abused. It's up to adults to recognise behaviours that make kids vulnerable to sexual abuse."[xx]

Child Protection Course

I always sensed that some of my early experiences of non-touching were still sexually abusive. This was validated and confirmed for me at the beginning of my studies in Early Childhood Education.

A requirement for completing my traineeship was to take a Child Protection Course through In Safe Hands. I was nervous that first night because I knew it would bring up lots of nightmarish stuff. In fact, there was a warning at the beginning of the course that it may be a trigger for survivors of childhood abuse. The course was a section labelled "Non-Contact Sexual Abuse."

I knew it! I knew that it was still sexual abuse even in the childhood experiences where there was no touching.

It was a moment of validation for me as a survivor.

Another moment of validation came when it described children who were sexually abused as having been treated as "worthless." It was the way Mum and my stepfather treated me, and the way my older sisters treated me. None of my "family" cared about me, not Mum, not my stepfather and not my sisters or they would have protected me.

The Chief Executive Officer of In Safe Hands was a man named Michael. He had nearly 30 years of experience in child protection case management, investigation and education. He had also served as a detective with the Queensland Police for twenty years investigating child abuse offences and was awarded the Assistant Commissioner's award for dedication to Child Protection.

After completing the course, I wanted so much to thank him for his work. I'm sure he is already aware of how much he has helped children, but he might not realise how much his work also helps adult survivors and their inner child too.

JOURNAL ENTRY 27 – THE PAEDOPHILE

A paedophile and misogynist, Quirky went from sexual comments to sexual activity with my mother in front of me. A malicious person who went out of his way to humiliate women and children, he took disturbing pleasure in causing fear and discomfort in a little girl.

I was sitting at the kitchen table eating cereal. My mum was sitting opposite me. Quirky's face was pasted to the news on television.

Suddenly, he stood up and walked behind my mother's chair. He massaged her shoulders.

While I was scooping the cereal and milk into my mouth, he told me, "Look at the television. Quick, look at the television." I tried to steady the spoon so as not to spill the cereal and looked at the television.

When I looked back to put my spoon back into my bowl, he had his hands on Mum's breasts. "Ooops. Ooops. Oh, oops. You just saw me touching your mother's private parts. "Oops," he said sarcastically with a sinister smirk. My stepfather was so morally repugnant to carry on like that in front of a child.

I was frightened and confused. I was just a child. I didn't know what to say or what to do. Now I can see that my stepfather's behaviour of sexualising my mother in front of me was laced with hate, misogyny and paedophilia. This is a form of gender-based violence against a woman and a little girl inflicted by a man. They should have been interacting and engaging with me in an age-appropriate manner by asking questions like, "What are you looking forward to at school today?" But he only cared about what was inside of his pants.

As for my mother, her face had no expression; she just looked dead behind the eyes. She just let him be disrespectful, not at all upset, shocked or angered by the way he mistreated me. What she didn't seem to realise was that he was disrespecting her too. It wasn't until I was an adult that I realised they were using me as sexual battery and a captive audience.

After that incident, I always disappeared into my bedroom while they were eating breakfast. After I heard my mother's car leave, I would tiptoe into the kitchen and make myself a bowl of cereal.

Quirky would say, "How come you wait until your mum leaves before you come out and eat breakfast?"

As if he didn't know!

The abuse continued because he knew my poor excuse of a mother had no boundaries and no intention of protecting me.

Definition of "Gender-based Violence": "Gender-based violence is a phenomenon deeply rooted in gender inequality and continues to be one of the most notable human rights violations within all societies. While both women and men experience gender-based violence, the majority of victims are women and girls. The Istanbul Convention acts of gender-based violence emphasised that such acts result in physical, sexual, psychological or economic harm or suffering to women, including threats of such acts, coercion or arbitrary deprivation of liberty, whether occurring in public or private life."[xxi]

Info Point: Modelling Respect and Appropriate Boundaries

"Children need to be treated with the same respect that is given to adults, and then some: keep explicit *adult* matters out of earshot or eyesight of children, as they are still *children*. The adults in a child's life need to take extra care when working to model good boundaries when it comes to privacy, touch, and other limits with a child. A child watches the important adults in their life, and if they see that it is okay when someone they love crosses the line with them, or in front of them, they will be more likely to think it's okay in other instances, which makes them more vulnerable to potential abuse."[xxii]

JOURNAL ENTRY 28 – NOT IN FRONT OF MY DAUGHTER

"You've been through a lot, you're one hell of a survivor, no dad, and an unreliable mum who had some not-so-nice boyfriends."

~ Unbelievable

Incidents continued of Quirky sexualising my mother in front of me.

We were on my parent's yacht. I was sitting with my mother and talking to her when Quirky came in, grabbed her T-shirt and looked down her shirt. Laughing, he looked at me and said, "I just looked down your mother's shirt." I remember he would always have a supercilious expression on his face when he looked at me. I was bewildered. Nothing is weaker or smaller than the man who hurts women and children, whether by his actions or words.

Mum didn't discourage him from this inappropriate activity. My mother should have told him that there is a time and place for everything and to save it for behind closed doors. She should have said, "Not in front of my daughter." She should have set boundaries.

Yet she had behaved this way with her boyfriends as well. One night, when she was involved with Melvin, I went to go to the bathroom. The door was closed, and I heard weird noises coming from the shower and my mother's laughter. I knew she was in the shower with Melvin. I was only four and that was confusing for me.

I ran through the house to look for my sister. Anne was in the lounge room doing her homework.

"Anne, why are Mummy and Melvin in the shower together? They're making weird noises."

Anne put her paper and pen down "Well ..." There was a long silence. "Well, sometimes big people do things together like taking showers together."

"Why?"

"Because they just do," she replied.

Later, I realised that a normal mother would have waited until her child was asleep. But my mother was too self-involved and focused on her pleasure to consider a child's needs.

JOURNAL ENTRY 29 – UNLOVED DAUGHTER: SEXUAL BATTERY

Quirky would masturbate my mother in front of me whenever he knew I was confined to the same space as them. One day, he parked at a petrol station. I was locked in the backseat of the car. My mother was in the front passenger seat.

While he was standing outside the car, he put his hand through the open window of the front passenger seat and masturbated my mother. While she made weird noises, he pressed his face up against my closed window and stared at me in the back seat with that sinister look. I'll never forget that evil look in his eyes. He was just demonic.

The look terrified me. Like a true paedophile, he seemed to get off on looking at me while he was sexualising her.

Having no escape is traumatic to say the least. They were supposed to be my caregivers, yet I was living with enemies. My "childhood" became an era of fear and sadness with a perpetual feeling of humiliation.

Info Point: "Purposely exposing a child to sexual acts *is* sexually abusive."[xxiii]

JOURNAL ENTRY 30 – EXPOSING HIMSELF

Quirky's inappropriate sexual behaviour went from fondling my mother in front of me (and talking sex to me) to exposing himself. The first time I remember was in a hotel.

My mother and I were sitting on the fold-out couch. Quirky was in the bathroom. He walked into the room, looked at me, smiled and took his pants down. Horrified, I ran out of the room shaking and hid in the bathroom.

My childhood was supposed to be my time to learn about respectful relationships and he stole that from me.

"One's childhood can be stolen through so many types of abuse, including sexual abuse. Sexual Abuse can be defined as exposing children to inappropriate sexuality through what they see, hear or experience. Childhood Sexual Abuse can happen through the overt actions of others or the failure to shield children from sexual content or behaviours."[xxiv]

Info Point: Exhibitionism

Exhibitionism is:

- a perversion in which sexual gratification is obtained from the indecent exposure of one's genitals

- an act of such exposure

- the act or practice of behaving to attract attention to oneself.

JOURNAL ENTRY 31 – SHROUDED IN SECRECY: CAPTIVE

One night my parents wanted a captive audience while they were having sex. They dragged me out of the bathroom and shut the bathroom door so I couldn't run back in. The bathroom had become my safe place.

Trapped, I cried, "LET ME OUT! LET ME OUT!" They just yelled at me to shut up. I crawled to the corner and wrapped myself into the fetal tuck.

During the day, they left me locked up and alone in the motel room, no food, no schooling, no company. Now at night they also traumatised me with sexual exhibitionism. Mum and Quirky were both shameless.

Child abuse is mostly a hidden crime. Imagine how alone I felt, so alone. Imagine how scary and overwhelming my little world felt. Childhood and sexual innocence were stolen from me.

Info Point: "The effects of sexual abuse extend far beyond childhood. Sexual abuse creates a loss of trust ... It can lead to antisocial behaviour, depression, identity confusion, loss of self-esteem and other serious emotional problems. It can also lead to difficulty with intimate relationships later in life. The sexual victimisation of children is ethically and morally wrong."[xxv]

JOURNAL ENTRY 32 – THE INTRUDER: STEPFATHER OR SEXUAL PREDATOR?

One day, in the playground at school, I shared with a friend during our lunch break the horrible things going on in my house. I knew she had a stepdad too and so she might understand.

"Mum and Stepdad do yucky things in front of me that make me feel gross. They make weird noises when they touch each other on their private parts. Does your stepdad do those things too?" I was hoping to find out if the things I was enduring were normal. I was trying to make sense of the senseless.

"My mum and stepdad don't do that," Ali said.

"Well then, what do they do?" I asked.

"They take me out for ice cream. We go to the park and the beach, and they take me to dancing lessons. We do fun things."

I felt crushed and lonely. I told her my mum and stepdad don't want to spend money on me for dancing lessons. They only wanted to spend money on their yacht and themselves. I could have asked my teacher this question, but because of Mum and Quirky, sometimes adults scared me. I couldn't trust them to answer me truthfully.

Also, from my own experience, I believe an abused child is more likely to disclose the abuse to a fellow child. It's easier to speak to someone the same size and stature than a big adult. And the teacher, overloaded and overworked with paperwork and large class sizes may not have the desire or inclination to take the time to establish a rapport with each student.

JOURNAL ENTRY 33 – CONTACT ABUSE

Eventually, Quirky moved from non-contact sexual abuse (sexualising Mum in front of me) to contact abuse. He would walk in on me in my bedroom and say, "I'll help you take off your clothes and change you into school clothes."

I would say, "No! I can do it myself" or "I want Mum."

He didn't listen but would forcefully undress me and look at me naked and touch me as I screamed out "MMMUUU-MMM!" Why did she never answer my cries for help?

He would also grab me and "tickle" me. He would also grab my arm and move his mouth up and down my arm, trying to kiss me all over my body. When I pulled away from him, distressed, he would say, "Oh I was only just playing and tickling you."

According to "Stop it Now," this pattern fits into how child sexual abuse often begins. Often, the perpetrator will start by "desensitizing" a child to certain types of inappropriate touching. They may do this by getting a child accustomed to roughhousing or play that includes brushing or touching genitals. They might push the envelope by repeating such behaviours in front of the child's parents or other adult caretakers to "test the waters" to see if the parents or other adults will notice and put a stop to such behaviours.

"When the adults do not put a stop to such behaviours, the potential sex abuser may begin to feel that they will be able to get away with abusing that child."[xxvi]

JOURNAL ENTRY 34 – GIRL INTERRUPTED

I was just out of kindergarten and in my first year of primary school when Quirky orally raped me.

I kept saying No repeatedly. I still remember how anxious I felt. I still remember how much I tried to stop the inevitable abuse that was about to occur. They didn't care about how many times I said No, all they cared about was coercive control. I kept trying to walk away from them to go back through the doorway to escape to my bedroom.

My poor excuse for a mother kept blocking the doorway.

"No," she said. "Stay here. I need your stepfather to look at you between your legs and make sure that everything is okay down there. He said he needs to do a medical check down there."

"Take me to a doctor," I said.

"No, I'm going to get your stepfather to look at it."

Terrified, I scratched the eczema on my neck and arms until it bled. I kept shaking my head and repeating, "No! No! No!" I tried to run out the door. Quirky blocked the doorway.

I remember my anxiety being at an all-time high. Hyper-vigilant, I kept looking back and forth between her and him, shaking my head and saying No.

My poor excuse of a mother kept screaming at me, "SAY YES! SAY YES, GYPSY! SAY YES!"

She kept blocking the doorway to hold me hostage in the Family Room. Deprivation of liberty.

"DO AS YOU ARE TOLD," my stepfather screamed at me as he always did throughout my childhood.

Narcissists have a very twisted and backward way of talking. My Mother asked, "Do you feel comfortable with this?" I answered, "No" and she then dictated with her reply and said, "No, say yes."

My own "mother" used me as some kind of sexual sacrifice and said to him, "Pull her pants down and look between her legs."

When I realised that my own mother wasn't going to protect me, I lost hope. They both cornered me, and I remember feeling so small and they were both so big. I still remember the trauma of not having a way out. I had tried both flight and fight and they both still overpowered me.

My stepfather overpowered me and exposed the bottom half of my body naked.

Children are easily overpowered.

He had no right to touch me there.

Quirky pulled my lips apart with his fingers and stared between my legs. He was on top of me and put his mouth on me down there. I was paralysed with fear, feeling helpless and powerless. I was under their control as he orally raped me, I remember clenching my fists.

While he was violating me, I called out to my mother and she refused to protect me. She just stood over me and stared. Can you imagine how horrific that must have been for me as a child? Can you imagine how horrific that memory must be for me as a woman?

I gave up on my mother and I left my body as a way to escape. I thought about the white horse, the one I had dreamt of. People who interfere with future generations are the worst kinds of people.

After my stepfather violated me, Mum said, "You can pull up your pants now." What followed were many sleepless nights.

Sometimes, I still have intrusive thoughts, I still remember how invaded I felt.

How ironic he orally raped me in a room called the "Family Room." There was no sense of family about them or that house. It was just a house of horrors.

Whenever I have flashbacks of those moments, I clench my fists remembering how powerless and helpless I felt in having no control over my body.

According to research, clenching fists is about willpower. It is a gesture associated with losing control. However, clenching your fist may help you get a grip on your emotions.

When I look back on my childhood, it's not just the traumatic events I see. It's also the absence of love, safety, respect and reverence. When I say "safety" I also mean feeling emotionally safe, not just physically safe.

Betrayal Trauma: "Betrayal Trauma is defined as a trauma perpetrated by someone with whom the victim is close to and reliant upon for support and survival. Betrayal Trauma Theory suggests that a child, being dependent on their caregiver for support, will have a higher need to dissociate traumatic experiences from conscious awareness."[xxvii]

Info Point: "Children cannot give permission; they are not consenting adults. Even if a child doesn't say No, it's still sexual abuse. Legally and morally, it's always the adult's responsibility to set boundaries with children and to stop the activity, regardless of 'permission' given by a child. Children cannot be responsible to determine what is abusive or inappropriate."[xxviii]

Info Point: "Most states recognise that children and teens can be easy to trick, easily persuaded, and raised to obey older youth or adults as authority figures. All of these factors explain why children and adolescents do not have the maturity, and therefore the legal right, to give informed consent."[xxix]

As a woman I absolutely adore living alone, no one can hurt me in my home anymore. My home is now my safe place, my sanctuary, living alone means so much to me.

JOURNAL ENTRY 35 – CHILD SEXUAL ABUSE DOES NOT HAVE TO INCLUDE PENETRATION

The sexual abuse continued. One night, my Stepfather came into my bedroom "to tuck me into bed." Terrified, I pulled the covers over my head. He pulled the covers down and touched me between my legs. I tried to pull away from him, but he used his body weight to hold me down.

Afterward, I ran into my sister Lynne's bedroom to tell her what happened. Lynne seemed unconcerned that he had violated me. "Maybe he accidentally touched you." Being almost ten years older than me, Lynn should have protected me. But she didn't. Nobody was defending me, not Lynne and not my mother. So Quirky continued to sexually abuse me.

Another time, I tried to tell my mother how I didn't like it when he came into my bedroom.

"I don't want him to tuck me into bed," I told her. "I want you!"

Quirky walked in and screamed, "I've never put my penis in you. I've never sexually abused you!"

It was true that he never put his penis inside me. But I still felt unsafe around him as a child.

Info Point: "To be considered child sexual abuse there does not have to be penetration to the vagina, anus, or mouth (by penis, tongue, finger or object), or involve force."[xxx]

JOURNAL ENTRY 36 – TOKOPHOBIA

Before that oral rape and after, I felt I didn't have a WAY OUT. Yet I had that precognitive dream about the white horse who told me I could use my mind to escape.

The impacts of abuse last a lifetime and my whole life has been consumed with having a WAY OUT. It's why I have never had any interest in marriage or having children because that kind of commitment is frightening, binding and entrapping. I would never want a child of my own because I would never want anybody to hurt them. Out of worry, I would be a helicopter mother and never let them out of my sight because I couldn't bear any harm coming to them.

My past has made me protective of children. They say children of narcissists are taught to hide their feelings and need for emotional support and to become someone who excessively cares for others but doesn't get their own needs met.

My calling to serve the world and help the children already here is bigger than the calling from my uterus wanting me to reproduce.

JOURNAL ENTRY 37 – THE NAUGHTIEST THING I DID AS A CHILD

One morning while I was sitting at my little dressing table, I looked at the box of bangles that belonged to my sister Lynne. I had never dared to even touch them because she had instructed me over and over, "DON'T touch my bangles. They're mine!"

Mum always bought nice things for Lynne, the Golden Child in her eyes. Sad that I wasn't also her Golden Child and having to put up with Quirky, who she just married, I picked up one of the pretty coloured bangles and placed it on my wrist hoping it would make me feel better.

I modelled it in front of the mirror and decided to wear it to kindy. Lynn had already left for school. She'll never know, I thought. I wasn't trying to be naughty. I just wanted to feel good. I wanted to be a child and play dress up.

At kindy, feeling snazzy with my bangle—well, my sister's bangle—I heard the bell ring for lunch. I paraded the bangle out to the oval. Suddenly I saw my sister with her friend walking toward me. Lynne waved at me and yelled, "Hi."

I turned and walked the other way to avoid them. But when I looked behind me, Lynne and her friend were running toward me. In hot pursuit, they were trying to catch up with me, so I took off running to the bathroom block.

I ploughed through the bathroom door and locked myself in one of the cubicles. Safe inside the cubicle, I tried to work out how to hide the bracelet I borrowed as I struggled to catch my breath. Well, kind of borrowed, borrowed without permission, if that makes sense.

The next thing I hear is banging on the door.

"Why are you running away from us?" Lynne demanded to know. "Open the door!"

I panicked and did the only thing I felt I could do in the heat of the moment. I took the bracelet off and flushed it down the toilet.

I opened the door. Lynne stared at me.

"Why were you running away from us?"

"I had to peepee," I lied. It was my first memory of lying.

"Oh, okay," she replied.

My sister stepped aside, and I sauntered back to the oval, bangle free and carefree. I enjoyed the rest of my lunch break in peace.

But when I returned to the classroom, that feeling of peace was disrupted. As my classmates and I were sitting on the floor and looking at our teacher, reading a storybook, there was a voice at the door.

We all turned around. A girl in the doorway said, "Sorry for the interruption. But someone reported a bangle in the bottom of the toilet that wouldn't flush. Does this belong to anyone in this classroom?"

I stared at her stunned, my mouth open and speechless. That bangle had come back to haunt me. I remained silent, thinking this was the best thing to do. *You have the right to remain silent otherwise anything you say or do can be held against you.*

Then, one of my kindy friends chimed in. "Gypsy, I saw you wearing that bracelet today."

Everybody turned to look at me.

"NNNNNOOOOOO!" I screamed. "No, I wasn't." Another lie.

"It's okay. You're not in trouble," said the girl at the doorway. "I just always like to return lost property. I went to a lot of trouble fishing it out of the toilet and washing it under the tap. It's clean."

She tried to reassure me as she stood there wearing gloves with that damn bangle in her gloved hands.

"NO! NO! NO! It's not mine!"

My kindy teacher interrupted, "Alright Gypsy. You don't need to get so upset about this."

Of course, I did. Inside my head were Melvin and Quirky's voices. "DON'T TELL!" They made me feel it wasn't safe to be honest, that I had to distrust people.

As I sat there mortified, my kindy teacher turned to the girl in the doorway and said, "She said it's not hers."

The girl with gloved hands replied, "Okay, well I thought I'd start with the kindy class. I'll go 'round to all the other classrooms to see who it belongs to."

"NNNNOOOO!!!!" I screamed out again.

My mind was racing. If she goes around to all the other classrooms, my sister will find out that I borrowed the bangle without asking.

"NNNOOOO!! DON'T go to all the other classrooms. It's been in the toilet. It's yucky! YUCKY! YUCKY! Put it in the bin!"

The kindy teacher reiterated this and said, "No one will want it after it's been in the toilet. Just chuck out the bangle."

"Okay," the gloved girl replied.

What sweet relief!

I don't remember ever hearing anything from Lynne about the bangle. So maybe the gloved girl did abort her plan of trying to return the bangle and just threw it in the bin.

Red Flag: Hiding things could be a sign of child abuse.

JOURNAL ENTRY 38 – DADDY ISSUES

I was playing in the sandpit. Playing next to me was this girl who kept going on about her daddy.

"Daddy?" That was a foreign word that I didn't recognise.

"What is a Daddy? I asked.

She looked at me quizzically.

"Everyone has one!"

I didn't. I had a *stepfather*.

Info Point: Fatherless daughter refers to the lack of an emotional bond between a daughter and her father due to various reasons including, but not limited to, death, divorce, abuse, addiction, incarceration or abandonment.

Research shows that as many as one in three women are considered fatherless and that losing the bond with their fathers deeply affected multiple areas of their lives, including their emotional and physical health.

Struggling with low self-esteem and unworthiness, these daughters are often not taught how to manage the trauma of their losses until later in life, when the woman re-experiences her pain and realises she has unresolved issues. The number one fear they had was being abandoned again. Most used isolation to cope. (*The Fatherless Daughter Project* by Karen Luise and Denna Babul.)

Some men use the word "Daddy Issues" as a victim-blaming insult against Fatherless Daughters. The phrase is sometimes used as a "joke" to humiliate women, for the mistreatment they suffered as a young girl. Of course, I was going to feel hurt by an absent biological father and an emotionally unavailable stepfather. Yet, it was these men who are actually the ones with the Daddy Issues.

I always wondered where my real father was, and why he never called or wrote. *Why didn't he want to see me?* He left when I was a baby and I had never met him. *Did he ever think about me?*

Later, I tried to track him down. I knew his name and I knew that he was a horse trainer and had his own horse farm. I found his phone number and called him. It went straight to voicemail. I left my number and told him it was my birthday soon. I said that I'd love to hear from him on my birthday as I'd had so many birthdays without him. He never called. I was devastated.

Eventually, he did leave me a text, a message that was his way of saying goodbye to me. "Some horses can't be tamed and maybe you're the same. I have a new family now, but I wish you the best."

I felt a lot of heartache, but I respected his wishes. Letting go of the emotionally unavailable man or father you never had is one of the hardest goodbyes.

JOURNAL ENTRY 39 – WALKING ON EGGSHELLS

I repeated something I heard Mum say, "The rainforest men are cute."

My poor excuse of a mother snapped, "Thanks a lot Gypsy. Thanks a lot!" Sulking, Quirky went quiet.

Mum always complained that Quirky looked at other women down the street, which he did. So why was she guilty about looking at other men down the street? If calling other men "cute" was so terrible, why was she saying it in front of her child?

Now I realise how ridiculous they both were. He was supposed to be a man, but he was a big baby, and she was always so overly concerned with massaging his ego while throwing an innocent child under the bus. They had never cared about me, but I was expected to always walk on eggshells with them.

Caregiver Tip: Children just repeat what they hear, they're not trying to cause trouble.

JOURNAL ENTRY 40 – NOT ALL IN THE FAMILY

Although Quirky was a heartless, nasty person, not everyone in his family was. His younger brother by two years was quite nice.

Many times, Quirky had dumped me with Mike several times a week. Mike would greet me with a smile and take me into the kitchen for something to eat. And not just leftovers.

He always behaved appropriately, never abusing me or sexualising his wife in front of me. She was also nice. They let me play with their three dogs and three cats who I loved very much.

At night, all the animals would sleep in my bed with me when I stayed in the spare bedroom. I was in heaven. My childhood may have been different if I had been able to stay there more often.

JOURNAL ENTRY 41 – LOVE IS PATIENT

One day my mum came home with a dress for me. I was so happy and excited because I wore the same hand-me-down clothes every day.

She said, "This is the dress you're going to wear to celebrate my wedding."

She seemed excited about me wearing my new dress to her wedding. I felt great hope in my heart. I thought, *She doesn't need to go to dances anymore to meet men. Now she has a man. She'll be happy and we can all be a family.*

On the day of the wedding, I met Quirky's three daughters and son. One big happy family.

Quirky and Mum thought the *Love is Patience* scripture would be great to include in the wedding vows—a "Grandiose Idea" indeed!—and requested that the priest repeat the scripture during the wedding vows.

During the wedding, the priest repeated it as requested and I listened intently.

"Love is Patient. Love is Kind. It does not envy, it does not boast, it is not proud. It is not rude, it is not self-seeking, it is not easily angered, it keeps no record of wrongs. Love does not delight in evil but rejoices with the truth. It always protects, always trusts, always hopes, always perseveres."[xxxi]

I loved it. I've always had a love for beautiful words, both spoken and written. I remember also being intrigued by how lovely the tables looked, with baby breadth blossom in small vases and all the name tags written in beautiful calligraphy.

Words and Actions Are Inconsistent

Of course, neither Mum nor my stepfather ever TRIED to live up to the *Love is Patient* scripture. Their actions were always contradictory to their words—another trait of narcissism. Though they claimed to love that scripture, they broke every word from it during their entire marriage! What a fiasco!

"If our words are not consistent with our actions, they will never be heard above the thunder of our deeds."

~ H. Burke Peterson

Info Point: Role Modelling: Your words have to be consistent with your actions. Children watch what you do and repeat your actions. At the early education centres where I've worked, if we wanted children to wear hats outside, we had to wear hats too.

JOURNAL ENTRY 42 – CONNECTION BEFORE CORRECTION

"I do not get along with those who do not know how to give a compliment or a word of encouragement."

~ Meryl Streep

Lynne only had to put up with Quirky for a very short time before she was old enough to move out. She first moved to Cairns, Queensland. There, she stayed with Misha. Lucky her. I would have moved out too if I was old enough.

During one of the very rare dinners Lynne had with us, Quirky gave a speech about how he's the head of the household and in control. "I'm the authority on everything," he said. "If anyone wants to leave the dinner table, it has to go through me. You have to ask for permission to be excused."

Typical narcissistic talk. Trying to control everyone and everything. A legend in his own lunchbox believing others should feel honoured to be in the presence of his grandiose greatness.

"WHOOPI-DO-DAH!" said Lynne.

I froze and looked at Quirky. He was staring at Lynne with murderous eyes.

I had a sore throat from feeling run down and covered my mouth with my hand, as I tried to clear my throat.

"You sound like a pig," my stepfather said to me. "Look at the way you're sitting, you're not sitting up straight enough. You're a disgrace!"

So pompous and pedantic. So excessively critical of me. Even my mother would laugh and say, "You're always criticizing my daughter."

They never wanted to see my light shine. Maybe if they could have spared a kind word here and there, my posture would not have looked so hunched and belittled. It's as if being cruel to me was a sport, a sinister game.

JOURNAL ENTRY 43 – LEARNING THROUGH PLAY

"There are no seven wonders of the world in the eyes of a child. There are seven million."

~ Walt Streightiff

"Learning through play" is a term used in early childhood education and psychology to describe how a child actively learns by interacting with the world. Through play, children develop social and cognitive skills, mature emotionally, and gain the self-confidence required to engage in new experiences and environments.

At home, I rarely played. Mum and Quirky didn't buy me toys. Often, I was alone with nothing to do. When I went to Grandma's house, I felt like a normal little girl whose day was filled with play.

One very fond memory was the time when Grandma, her cat Jaimie and I were playing in the garden and found a Ladybird (often called Ladybug).

The Ladybird flew off the flower and onto my hand.

"Oh, look Grandma!" Then the Ladybird flew back to the flower.

"It's good luck when you see a Ladybird," Grandma said to me. Grandma knew her stuff. Some cultures believe seeing a Ladybug does bring good luck and the person may succeed in love, enjoy good weather, experience financial success, or have a wish come true.[xxxii]

"Grandmas hold our tiny hands for just a little while but our hearts forever."

~ Unknown

My grandma took good care of me. She fed me, breakfast, lunch, dinner and snacks. She would sit down with me and drink endless cups of tea. She would talk to me and be interested in what I had to say. I always slept well at her home. I wasn't hypervigilant as I was at home because I felt safe, secure and supported.

She gave me a safe space to be a child. We were in the lounge room admiring how cute Jaimie the cat was. Grandma taught me that when a cat's nose is wet, it's a sign of health. *She taught me things and I loved it! Mum and Quirky were never educational, just abusive.*

One time when we had tea together, she taught me, "If you leave the spoon in your cup the heat will travel up the spoon and into the air." (A metal spoon in a cup of tea will act as a radiator, conducting heat to the air.) I've always remembered that.

Grandma, Jaimie and I would work in her garden at the back of the house. Sometimes, Jaimie would wander off. When it was time for Jaimie's dinner, Grandma and I would go to the front of the house and Grandma would hit the spoon against a can of cat food. *Ding, ding, ding.* That was Jaimie's signal that it was dinnertime. He would run up the stairs and into the house.

Grandma was beautiful, her home was beautiful, and her cat was beautiful. I wish I had the money to buy that house. It's a special home where the happiest memories of my childhood took place—Grandma, Jaimie and me, all three of us.

It was Grandma and Jaimie that made that home special. She made sure that the two of us had a photo together and that

Jaimie and I had a photo too, that I still cherish to this day. She made me feel special and seen.

Grandma stuck up for me too.

Sometimes, Lynne and I both went together to Grandma's house. Because I was the baby sister, Lynne would take advantage and bully me. She knew she was Mum's favourite, her "Golden Child," and Mum wouldn't disapprove. Because she had grown up watching Mum being mean to me, she learned that was how she was supposed to behave to the "unwanted" child.

One time when we were at Grandma's house, Lynne said in her usual aggressive manner, "You DON'T leave your teaspoon in your teacup, Gypsy!"

"It's Gypsy's teacup. She can leave her spoon in there if she wants," Grandma said in defence of me in her soft, sweet voice that I loved. I felt so protected since my mother never defended me against Quirky's assaults.

All of my memories in that house were idyllic! I felt so fulfilled and at peace. I'll always remember the beautiful furry cuddles from Jaimie and how he looked at me with those magical feline eyes, and the way he purred when he slept on my lap and the respectful way my Grandma spoke to me. She never called me bad names. She always had so much reverence and respect. A wonderful woman, she never mocked me. She was Grace Incarnate.

I hold the memory of both Grandma and Jaimie so close to my heart. When I light Rose Musk incense, I remember the rose garden at her house. All the wonderful memories come flooding back.

The garden called Paradiso Perduto ("Lost Paradise" in Italian) from the movie *Great Expectations*, reminds me of my grandma's garden. As I write this, I wish she were still alive. She's very much alive inside me and through my memory of her. If only I could visit her, even just one more time, to sit and have tea with her and her cat Jaimie, to laugh and play like we used to.

Convention on the Rights of the Child, Article 31. Children have the right to relax, play and to join in a wide range of leisure activities.[xxxiii]

JOURNAL ENTRY 44 – RAPUNZEL

One day my mum walked into my bedroom and found me brushing my hair in front of the mirror. She started screaming at me, "You look a mess and your hair looks a mess." She grabbed the hairbrush off of me and started ripping it through my hair.

"You're hurting me, stop!" I cried.

"You look a mess with all that eczema all over your neck and arms." She was critical of me as usual. "I'm going to cut off your hair. It's all tangled."

"Noooo. Please don't cut my hair," I pleaded.

Ignoring me, she grabbed the scissors and cut off all of my hair as I sobbed.

Laughing she said, "Now you look like a boy!"

I've never forgotten that and, to this day, I've always loved having long hair.

One evening, I overheard Mum say, "Lynne is my favourite child. When she was born, I felt that a star was born!"

I was actually glad to hear this. I finally thought it makes sense that she always treats Lynne better than me.

JOURNAL ENTRY 45 – I KNOW WHY THE CAGED BIRD SINGS

"The greatness of a nation and its moral progress can be judged by the way its animals are treated."

~ Mahatma Gandhi

As an Early Childhood Educator, I learned the importance of limiting the use of "No's" and "Don'ts" because it's important, within reason, for children to receive positive affirmation.

My childhood was filled with "No's" and "Don'ts."

I had begged Mum and Quirky yet again for a cat or a dog. They said "No" yet again. They always loved saying the word No to me: No to animals; No to dancing lessons; No to everything. But Yes to their yacht and Yes to all their things.

It was hard going to school and hearing about all the dancing, gymnastic, piano and tennis lessons and other fun things that other girls received.

I said to Mum and Stepfather, "I'm not asking for everything that other girls get. I'm just asking for one thing," I pleaded. "Can't you give me one dancing lesson per week or a cat or a dog?"

Quirky laughed and said, "I'd be happy to get you a bird in a cage."

"But I want something to cuddle. I want a cat or a dog."

Quirky screamed, "You're getting a caged bird or nothing at all!"

The next day he brought home a caged bird. I took the bird out of the cage and patted him and let him fly around the house, before putting him back in the cage. I carried this cage everywhere with me. Quirky smirked and sniggered every time he saw me carrying around the bird in the cage.

Misha and her boyfriend Paul visited one day. Paul put his face up to the cage. He started saying mean things to the bird. I stared at him horrified.

"STOP IT, STOP SAYING THAT!" I cried.

"Oh, he doesn't know what I'm saying. You can say really mean things in a nice tone of voice, and the animal will never know! That's what's so funny about animals!" He gloated, laughing and sniggering. It was like he was a carbon copy of Quirky.

"I don't like it!" I cried.

I didn't like Paul anymore. I didn't feel safe and I felt scared for my bird. I grabbed the cage and carried my bird to the safety of my bedroom.

I sang the song "The Horses" by Daryl Braithwaite to my caged bird.

My bird chirped back when I sang to him.

Even in a cage, your corner of freedom is how you choose to think.

During the captivity of my childhood, my corner of freedom was my imagination and my mind, the way I chose to think.

Like me, that bird shouldn't have been within the confinements of that cage. The way out of that cage is to share your story if you feel safe and hear other people's stories too.

I turned to the wonderful world of art and books to get my needs and wants met.

Singing that song "The Horses" helped me to escape.

I was so glad when my sister Misha and her boyfriend Paul left. I already had enough bullies to deal with in Mum and Quirky. I didn't need to deal with any more bullies.

JOURNAL ENTRY 46 – GASLIGHTING

Weeks later, after Quirky bought me the bird, I came home from school to find a different bird in the cage.

I ran into the kitchen and asked Mum and Quirky, "Why did you put a different bird in there? Where's my other bird? Where's Pepper?"

Mum laughed. "Gypsy, you're so silly. What are you talking about? That is Pepper!"

"I'M NOT SILLY and no, it's not Pepper! He looks slimmer than Pepper and his feathers are lighter blue and more white than Pepper."

"Oh well. Sometimes bird's feathers fall off and they change colour," my Mother laughed in reply.

I turned to Quirky. "That's not the same bird, is it?"

He shrugged his shoulders and said nothing, a smirk on his face.

"He looks like he lost weight. He couldn't have lost that much weight in one day!"

Mum and Quirky smirked and sniggered but said nothing.

"You're both acting funny. Why can't you tell me what happened to my baby bird?"

Angry now, my mother yelled, "You're too sensitive, Gypsy. I've always told you that you're too sensitive! That's your problem. You're too sensitive!"

The caged bird chirped as if to interrupt.

"DID YOU HEAR THAT?" I demanded. "His voice is different from Pepper's. That's not Pepper's voice! WHAT DID YOU DO WITH MY BIRD? WHAT DID YOU DO TO PEPPER? WHY HAVE YOU PUT A DIFFERENT BIRD IN THIS CAGE? WHERE'S PEPPER?"

"You think too much, Gypsy! You're crazy, Gypsy!" my mother yelled back at me.

Confused, disoriented, I burst into tears. I was certain that it was not the same bird. Yet, Mum and Quirky were colluding and denying my reality.

When I went to bed that night, I crept out to stand near the doorway of the lounge room for hours. I could hear Mum and Quirky talking while they were watching TV.

Quirky said, "Your daughter knows that it's not the same bird. She knows you're lying to her."

"Well, I'm not telling her that I took the cage outside," said Mum. "I didn't know that a magpie was going to open the cage door and let the budgie out. I know what Gypsy is like over animals. She'll start crying and I can't be bothered dealing with her and her emotions. I don't have the patience for her."

There was no need for me to keep listening. I had my answer. I was still hurting but I didn't feel as confused.

I crept back to bed and cried. *She doesn't have the patience for me*, I thought, and then remembered the *Love is Patient* scripture read at their wedding. She doesn't love me or she would have patience with me, she would have told me the truth about my bird and helped me to grieve the loss. But she didn't care about me and my feelings. I cried myself to sleep.

"All the reading she had done had given her a view of life that they had never seen. If only they would read a little

Dickens or Kipling they would soon discover there was more to life than cheating people and watching television."

~ Roald Dahl

JOURNAL ENTRY 47 – VIOLENCE IS NOT THE ANSWER

One day, when I was 13 years old, I looked out the window and said, "I love all this rain. It's so beautiful."

Paul, Misha's boyfriend, attacked me relentlessly. "Oh, if you like the rain then that makes you miserable! You're miserable just like the rain!"

Previously, he'd laughed when I fell down the stairs and injured my ankle. On another occasion, he called me a pig while I was eating. In yet another incident, he tried to triangulate me with my sister by saying that he would have to use photoshop to make me look attractive and then added that Misha was naturally a babe. Paul was playing me off against my sister and Misha gloated, letting him disrespect me.

"Please stop being so mean to me," I pleaded, sick and tired of all of his verbal violence that he hurled at me.

"I could say worse to you," Paul said. "I could say so many things to you that would make you cry." That comment said more about him than it did about me.

Chiming in, Misha said, "You provoked Paul, Gypsy! You provoked him!"

Really? A young girl provoking a grown man because I was begging for kindness? Wow, Misha and Paul were both really a piece of work, a truly pathetic couple. So immature.

Mum and Quirky disappeared to sail around Australia for almost a year and had given Misha a car and money to look after me. Yet, Misha was still mean and resentful toward me.

All three of my sisters were. Excluding me, they referred to themselves as "Orion's Belt" star constellation, "The Three Stars."

After Misha married Paul, she complained that he became crueler and crueler. Misha was okay when his cruelty was directed at me. But not now when it was finally directed toward her.

Paul quit his job right after their honeymoon and, for many years lived off my sister's income. On top of this, Misha discovered he relentlessly watched porn in his study every night. "Now it makes sense why he never wants to have sex with me," Misha said.

When they finally had children, Misha told her husband she doesn't believe in smacking children, asking him not to hit them. One day, when Misha was out and Mum was there, she witnessed Paul giving one of Misha's son's a big WHACK! Paul's lack of respect for his wife and their children upset Misha greatly.

JOURNAL ENTRY 48 – ISOLATION

When I was 14 years old, I went to an all-girls school. My stepfather had said he didn't want any boys around me.

I used to tape dancing shows like *Burn the Floor*, a source of great joy and happiness for me. Quirky would walk past and make snide comments. "Do they do any different dances after you've watched it one hundred times?"

One day, I accidentally taped over one of his favourite movies. He had hundreds of other taped movies in his collection. I thought it was a spare tape as it was the only one without a label. Afterward, he confronted me and vengefully taped over both of my dancing videos. Vindictive as always, he took away those little pieces of happiness that helped me to cope.

They wouldn't let me have dancing lessons, though I eventually paid for my own when I was old enough to work. They wouldn't let me have friends. They wouldn't let me go to camp.

Finally, my religion teacher stepped in, concerned at how distressed I was at school. Crying, I told him that they never let me go over to my friend's places or go to camp.

He confronted my stepfather and told him that friendships are important. My religion teacher was taller and bigger than my stepfather and my stepfather cowered in his presence. Though I can't remember the religion teacher's name, I will always be grateful for his help and standing up to Quirky.

JOURNAL ENTRY 49 – DOWN THE RABBIT HOLE

"Power is being told you are not loved and not being destroyed by it."

~ Madonna

When I was 12 years old, I first talked about wanting to end the pain I was living. Yet again I had been absent from schooling for months. After pleading for dancing lessons since the age of seven, and constantly being told "No," life felt hopeless. And of course, there was the constant ongoing abuse, exhausting me emotionally. To say my childhood was "deprived" was an understatement.

"I've got nothing to live for," I told my mother. "You've got your husband and I've got nobody and nothing."

I had seen an episode of Oprah where the topic was about who would you save, your partner or your children? I already had my answer from personal experience. I knew that she would save her husband and not me. I had no meaning in my life and saw no reason to go on living. I just wanted to end my life.

When I was 15 years old, I made a suicide attempt. My girlfriends had talked about how they'd heard through their parents and the media about how to escape the pain.

"How?" I asked.

"Alcohol."

With my girlfriends, I drank down many bottles of alcohol. I lost all memory of my behaviour. Later, they told me that I was crashing around their place and trashing it. Not knowing what to do with me, they grabbed my arm and walked me down the street. "Maybe we should take her back to the house and lay her on the bathroom floor, under a freezing cold shower," I remember vaguely one voice saying.

The floor on the street was moving.

"Look at the floor," I pointed out.

I remember one of their voices saying, "It's pretty, isn't it?"

Next, a doctor walked by and turned me on my side. I was on the floor choking on my own vomit. He stuck his hand down my throat to clear all the vomit out of my mouth, to stop me from choking to death.

The next thing I recall was being in the ambulance. I saw oxygen masks and knew that I needed saving. So, I grabbed one of the oxygen masks and held it against my face. My survival instincts had finally kicked in. However ludicrous it looked I really was trying to save myself.

That's when the paramedic panicked. I remember his face was so blurry and his face kept moving. "What did you give her? You're not in trouble as long as you tell me what you gave her and how much. I need to know so that I can help her."

My friend finally told him how much alcohol I'd had. Just like my childhood had been in the hands of Mum and Quirky, my life was now in the hands of this paramedic. I let go, dropped the oxygen mask and blacked out on the ambulance floor.

I woke up. Attached to my arms were so many wires and tubes, along with two drips and other paraphernalia.

I called out, "MMMMUUUUMMM." There was a deafening silence. Again, I called out, "MMMMUUUUMMM."

A nurse walked in. "We've contacted your mum. We've told her that you're here.

"Then why isn't she here?" I asked. There was silence and so I answered the question myself. "She never wanted me," I told the nurse. "I wasn't wanted."

The nurse replied, "I'll call her again." I closed my eyes to see darkness and fell back asleep.

I heard voices. "Well, we weren't sure at first whether she'd make it through," said the doctor. I opened my eyes to Quirky sitting on a chair at the foot of the bed, looking aloof and reading a newspaper.

Mum was standing next to him listening to the doctor. In a firm voice, he told them, "I can see that you both feel inconvenienced by all of this. But you should be glad that your daughter is a survivor. Not everyone can survive something like this. Please be grateful that she pulled through."

It was sadly surreal, that a doctor had to explain to a mother and stepfather that you're supposed to be grateful when your child survives.

My stepfather lifted his head from the newspaper and chimed in, "She's not my daughter." Mother just shrugged.

"I knew I belonged to the public and the world, not because I was talented or even beautiful, but because I had never belonged to anything or anyone else."

~ Marilyn Monroe

I thought about the doctor's words. He called me a survivor. Yet, I'm not sure if my ability to trust had survived. Maybe there was a reason I was still here. Maybe there was still something inside of me to be shared. The bravest thing I ever did was continue to live when all I wanted to do was die.

JOURNAL ENTRY 50 – IT'S ALL ABOUT HER

After my suicide attempt, I worked hard to rebuild my life and to establish a relationship with my mother.

One evening, I brought Mum with me to see my school friends, so she didn't have to be alone on New Year's Eve. She was going through a divorce and I was worried about her wellbeing and welfare. I even asked my friends, "Why don't you invite your parents to come with us too and watch the fireworks with us?" A few of them agreed to this when I added, "Family is everything!"

When I turned Sweet Sixteen, my Mother was almost sixty and alone. I said to her, "We never had a mother-daughter relationship when I was growing up and I'm upset about that. Let's change that. I want you to come to my Latin-American dance classes with me."

She was reluctant and so I used men to convince her to spend some family time with me. I added, "If you go to dancing lessons with me, you might just meet your next husband there!" This convinced her to spend some family time with me. "Should we go see one of the new releases at the movies sometime? We should have a mother-daughter day this Saturday!"

"I know how desperate you are to try and rebuild our mother-daughter relationship. But I want to be available if one of my boyfriends decide to see me," mother said and declined.

"Okay, fine. I understand." I replied. She didn't have it in her to be a mother to me. She was too self-involved.

JOURNAL ENTRY 51 – SWEET SIXTEEN & SABOTAGE

Now that Quirky and my mother were divorced, he no longer wanted to pay for my tuition at the all-girls college. I started seeing a boy from the new high school I was going to—the first boy I had fallen for, the first boy I felt romantic about.

I shared this with my mother and told her that I'd like her to meet his family one day, still forever trying to get my mother to be involved and interested in my life, desperately needing an open, honest, healthy family relationship with her.

After spending the day with my boyfriend and meeting his parents, I invited them inside when they drove me back home. I introduced him and his parents to my mother. We all sat down and talked.

My mother sneakily said, "Oh I better get your phone number off of you just in case I ever need to know where my daughter is." I was to find out that my poor excuse for a mother was not just a slut but a premeditated slut.

My boyfriend and his family left. The next night I went out to dancing lessons with my girlfriend and invited my mother too. She declined.

When I returned home later that night, I heard a man cough and my gut instinct told me it was my boyfriend's dad. Sure enough, as I walked out of the kitchen, I saw my boyfriend's dad walking out of my mother's bedroom and down the stairs.

My mother walked out of her bedroom looking disappointed and angry. (I later learned why, when I overheard her complaining to a friend that he had a tiny prick.) When she saw me, she had a sadistic smirk on her face and bullied me relentlessly.

She laughed and gloatingly ranted, "I just slept with the father of your boyfriend. How do you like that? If I was your age, you better watch out because I'd be sleeping with your boyfriend instead! Even though I'm not your age I can still ruin things between you and your boyfriend. I could try to marry his dad and make you and your boyfriend stepbrother and stepsister."

I collapsed on the couch in tears. I was crying uncontrollably, so much so that I was shaking. I stared at her in disbelief through a flood of tears. The one person who was supposed to be supporting me, supporting my life and relationships was instead trying to destroy it all. After I had been working so hard to rebuild my life after an attempted suicide, she does this to me. I was drowning, I was never taught to swim as a child. This is why I was struggling to keep my head above water. Every time I reached out for the lifeboat my mother would keep kicking my hand away. I was speechless and still shaking and crying. I looked at her in disbelief as her relentless ranting continued.

"I think I've already done a good job of ruining it between you and your boyfriend. Your boyfriend's dad will never take you seriously as a girlfriend for his son. Plus, your boyfriend won't take you seriously now either." She walked off and left me there on the couch crying uncontrollably.

Why did she always find it so difficult for her attitude to go from "me" to "us." She knows that she could have a one-night stand with anybody. It didn't have to be the father of my boyfriend. My poor excuse for a mother would always draw a very clear line in the sand when it came to HER people, HER life, HER belongings, HER food, HER bedroom, HER mirror. She wouldn't even let me brush my hair in front of her mirror and she wouldn't give me a mirror for my bedroom. Yet, she felt entitled to invade my life. The motto of a narcissistic mother or narcissist in general is: "What's mine is mine and what's yours is mine too!" It's a very toxic attitude to have within a relationship.

Self-entitled, she said, "Oh well, the father of your boyfriend and I are two consenting adults. It's about two consenting adults." I replied through tears, "It is about two consenting adults but not in this situation. You know you've crossed the line. How could you? You know how hard I've tried to have a good relationship with you."

"Never feel ashamed that you could not save the relationship that someone else deliberately destroyed and threw away."

~ Unknown

"Some people can recognise a tree, a front yard, and know they've made it home. How many circles can I walk in before I give up looking? How long before I'm lost for good."

~ *13 Reasons Why*

JOURNAL ENTRY 52 – TO LOVE AND BE LOVED IN RETURN

After I read Jane Eyre, I learned that Charlotte Bronte had to use a pen name, a male pseudonym, to avoid being viewed with prejudice. I decided to do the same to get a cat. After many years of asking my stepfather for a cat and being told No, I decided to approach his brother who was so nice.

"Please ask my stepfather to get me a cat. He will take it seriously if the request comes from you and not from me."

It worked like magic!

When I adopted Michael as a kitten, the lady there asked me: "What are you going to do during the school holidays?"

"I'm going to spend time with my kitten."

"I thought so," she smiled back at me.

I brought my baby back home and cuddled him close. So happy to have such love after all the hatred I had endured from my abusive parents. From the hateful misogynistic violence from my stepfather to being bullied by boys at school for my fair skin.

Finally, at 14 years old I had a bundle of furry love in my arms, a sentient creature in my arms to love and he loved me back.

We would play together. He was so intelligent he could actually play fetch. I would throw little cat toys and he would run and fetch it and bring it back to me. My bedroom door was a sliding door and he would use his paw to slide it open to visit me in my bedroom.

I was so impressed with him. My childhood companion, we would sleep together and after school I would always look forward to coming home to him.

Besides dancing, I thought I had found something else I was good at: being a Cat Mother.

Yet, I feel like I failed at that after turning sixteen and falling into a debilitating depression at the hands of my own mother's nastiness.

JOURNAL ENTRY 53 – DEBILITATING DEPRESSION

"You will be required to deny yourself: your hopes, your dreams, your fears, your aspirations, your emotional needs, and sometimes your material needs. You will be asked to deny reality and ignore it. It is very disorientating. Most victims feel that they are going crazy or that they are guilty of something obscure, opaque and ominous. It is Kafkaesque: an endless, ongoing trial without clear laws, known procedures, identified judges. It is nightmarish."

~ Sam Vatkin

After her betrayal with my boyfriend's father, I suffered debilitating depression and felt I had nothing to live for. Also, being pulled in and out of so many different schools was the last straw. I started thinking about suicide again. I started feeling regret that I had survived that first suicide attempt. I wasn't coping. I wasn't functioning. Just getting out of bed to get a bowl of cereal was a huge effort.

Plus, there was barely any food in the house because my mother kept most of the food locked away in her bedroom. Old habits die hard. She started taking my government youth allowance off me. She said that she wanted to buy breast implants for herself and that I should start working full-time instead of one shift per week, to give her extra money to support herself.

I tried to reason with her. "How will I ever have time to focus on school if I have to work full-time to support you?"

Plus, every day she would tear me apart and tell me I was ugly and fat and any other criticism she could come up with. She would pinch my skin and say, "See? Look at how fat you are! No man would ever want you!"

I came home from school one day feeling hopeless and helpless. I had forced myself to go to school feeling depressed. When I walked inside, I was tired from the hour-long walk home from the bus stop. Of course, my mother had to pick a home for us that was hours away from civilisation. She didn't care about the impact on me because she had a car.

I dropped my school bag on the floor and collapsed on the floor. I had given up on life. I heard my cat Michael's meows from the laundry in the garden. I had him since I was fourteen.

Why did my Mother lock him away inside after I went to school? It was as if she was treating him the way she treated me when I was a child. I could still hear Michael's meows, but my depression was so debilitating that I couldn't even move and get up off the floor.

Since he was a kitten, Michael and I were a beautiful mutual source of love and joy to each other. Yet I was feeling too helpless and hopeless to move.

Suicide had been dominating my thoughts again because my mother made me feel I wasn't even good enough to be alive. I turned on some music in a desperate attempt to be outside of myself. It didn't work. I turned on the TV. That didn't work and I turned everything off and collapsed back down on the floor.

Later, when my mother came home from work that day, I told her, "You have to give Michael away. It's not fair that you're locking him in the laundry while I'm at school. It's mean."

She had a shocked look on her face.

"I know it's dangerous for him to be outside without us, as he might get run over. But it's mean that you won't let him stay inside the house during the day. The laundry is too small for him to be locked inside all day."

She argued that this house wasn't as big as the other house and that she needed to keep his litter and food locked away in the laundry with him.

"This place is a hellhole and he deserves better. He deserves a better home."

Though still depressed, I wanted to fight for Michael to have a better home and to have a better life. Michael would be better off with anyone than with me.

And so, my mother gave Michael back to the shelter to be re-homed. My source of love and joy that I had raised since a kitten was now gone. I loved him so much.

We went to visit him at his new home. He was with a lovely couple. I gasped in shock when I saw him though.

"What happened to his tail?" I asked.

"He was hit by a car and his tail was injured. We took him to the vet, but they could only do so much. We don't believe in keeping cats inside all day. We think they should be allowed to walk free outdoors."

I went to pat him, but he ran away from me.

"Okay, fine then," I said and walked away.

Michael then ran back to me and I gave him lots of cuddles. I told him how much I loved him and reluctantly said goodbye.

I missed him so I felt like I was running on empty without him, as if a part of me had been wiped out without him. I pined for him and for the mother I never had. In place of a mother was just a beyond bitchy, satanic slut who bullied and threatened me relentlessly every day.

One morning, I dreamed that Michael opened my bedroom door with his paw and jumped on my bed. When I woke up, I started to search around my bed for Michael. Then I realised it was just a dream and that I no longer had Michael. It felt like a hallucination. I believe this was a visitation dream and his spirit was trying to comfort mine, that Michael the beautiful cat, my baby, wanted so much to be with me because he knew I was going through hell. Cats are very clairvoyant.

We had a special connection and shared something precious. I raised him for years since he was a kitten and I gave him lots of affection for two and a half years. But towards the end, I was struggling with life too much to take care of him. I had even stopped dancing and writing. I was absent from school due to extended bouts of sadness and eventually, I dropped out of high school.

I hope he knows how much I loved him but that I was just a lost little girl.

My burgeoning womanhood was built on top of a childhood that hadn't had any foundation. You know what they say about buildings without a foundation, they come crashing down.

JOURNAL ENTRY 54 – LIBRARY WAS MY LIFELINE

Thank goodness for books and the wonderful world of art for saving my life, during primary school and onwards!

To cope with my family with neither Mum, Quirky, Misha, Anne or Lynne wanting nor making the effort to have meaningful interactions with me—they were either nasty or ignored me as if I were invisible—the library became my lifeline: I had relationships with books.

Though my mother and stepfather were never there for me, books were! I learned about healthy relationships, emotions, values, morals and love through books, instead of my "caregivers."

One of my favourites is the tales of King Arthur and the Knights of the Round Table. Discovered this legend at age 8!

Why King Arthur chose a round table always resonated with me. A round table has no head of the table and reminds us that we are all equals.

How beautiful. A story about respect! These were the stories my soul needed as a child; I was in heaven! I was with them when all the Knights of King Arthur's Round Table took their oath.

This is part of the oath and should be for all of us to take to heart:

"I will develop my life for the greater good. I will place character above riches, and concern for others above personal wealth … I will speak the truth at all times, and forever keep my word. I will defend those who cannot defend themselves, I will honour and respect women, and refute sexism in all its guises, I will uphold justice by being

fair to all, I will be faithful in love and loyal in friendship ...
I will be generous to the poor and to those who need help. I
will forgive when asked, that my own mistakes will be
forgiven, I will live my life with courtesy and honour from
this day forward."

~ King Arthur, *Le Morted'Arthur: King Arthur and the*
Legends of the Round Table

The part about honouring and respecting women and being
fair to all resounds within me and gave me hope that not all
men were disrespectful cowards like Quirky.

Then there was the *Song of the Lioness* series by Tamora
Pierce which I devoured. It was set in medieval times just like
the tales of King Arthur and the Knights of the Round Table.
The main character was a female knight. I was thrilled! It felt
like Pierce wrote this just for me. I think Pierce was one of
my very first teachers in feminism. Alanna was a heroine
courageous enough to challenge the status quo!

When I finished the first book about Alanna, I cried because I
felt like I was grieving the end of a relationship. I couldn't
wait until I could read the rest of the series. Engaging with
the many different characters within a book helped me to
forget the reality of my traumatic relationships, or should I
say lack of relationship with Mum and Quirky.

"So Matilda's strong young mind continued to grow,
nurtured by the voices of all those authors who had sent
their books out into the world like ships on the sea. These
books gave Matilda a hopeful and comforting message: You
are not alone."

~ Roald Dahl, *Matilda*

I read *Matilda* by Roald Dahl relatively late in childhood. It really resonated with me and I felt as if he was talking directly to me, as if the author had observed my childhood and was describing it back to me.

"Sometimes Matilda longed for a friend, someone like the kind, courageous people in her books."

~ Roald Dahl, *Matilda*

I started to write to Australian Author Roseanne Hawke after reading her books, and she would write back! Even though my stepfather would always shout at me, "DON'T GET YOUR HOPES UP!"

JOURNAL ENTRY 55 – CONNECTION THROUGH CHESS

"What she needed was just one person, one wise and sympathetic grown-up who could help her."

~ Roald Dahl, *Matilda*[xxxiv]

At 7 years old, I went to the local library after school, I would see a man there, maybe 70 or 75, who volunteered his time. He had a kind face and sat at a table with a chessboard. He would teach and play chess with any child who wanted to learn. Maybe this is why I hold chess so close to my heart.

Week after week, he taught me about chess, how the Queen is the most important piece, how the knight moves in an L direction. Those memories I had with him were idyllic and I learned a love of chess.

Caregiver Tip: "Chess is a great game to teach your children for many reasons. It helps children develop their spatial skills, improves memory, helps them use both sides of their brain, improves IQ and social skills."[xxxv]

JOURNAL ENTRY 56 – LOVE WITHOUT A MAP

"When we wrote To the Moon and back ... I always felt people would connect with the lyric and the emotion of the music"

~ Daniel Jones, *Savage Garden*

People should enter adulthood ready to take on the world. I walked away from childhood confused, insecure about my future, and my ability to attract loving people into my life.

Going back to my metaphor, I felt like a captive whale who gets released back into the big wide world with a faulty sonar system. As a result, the whale is unable to navigate the oceans and constantly ends up beached in shallow locations.

As a Piscean Mermaid who had not yet been empowered with echolocation, I was struggling to navigate the ocean. Instead of avoiding an abusive relationship, I found myself plunging through the dangerously shallow and stormy seas of domestic violence having, not surprisingly, attracted an abusive boyfriend—a man incapable of loving me back.

Violence starts with disrespect. That a man would disrespect me was inevitable since Mum and Quirky had disrespected me. Nor did they role model a map on what a respectful relationship looks like. An educated empath is a narcissist's worst nightmare.

In order to heal, I had to create my own sanctuary by re-parenting myself. When I empowered myself through education, I was like a Mermaid learning about echolocation and how to navigate.

"I must be a mermaid. I have no fear of depths and a great fear of shallow living."

~ Anais Nin

How do we protect ourselves against domestic violence?

Education!

"Education is the movement from darkness to light!"

~ Allan Bloom

And love.

"If you want to change the world, go home and love your family."

~ Mother Theresa

JOURNAL ENTRY 57 – COMMITMENT PHOBIC

When most people see a wedding they tend to think, *What a wonderful celebration of commitment.* When I see a wedding, like when I see a bride and groom stroll out of a church, I cringe. Yet, I can't help but stare with the frightened eyes of my inner child. It's like trying to tear your eyes away from a train wreck. I ask myself, *Will the man abuse the woman? Will they abuse their child? What dark path will this commitment lead to?*

I have a similar frightening feeling when I see a pregnant woman.

"Pause you who read this and think for a moment of the long chain of iron or gold, of thorns or flowers, that would never have bound you, but for the formation of the first link on one memorable day."

~ Charles Dickens, *Great Expectations*

I remember when I was a flower girl for my mother and stepfather's wedding. At that time, I was only five. If I had been older my head would have raced with lots of questions.

How many arguments will they have?

How ugly will the arguments get?

Will he try to control her by controlling all the finances?

Is he just marrying her because she's a single mum and he wants to prey on her daughter?

What kind of impact will the marriage have on me?

Will I grow up to be promiscuous or will I be celibate and avoid relationships?

How long will it be before he has an affair?

How long will it be before they get divorced? How bitter will the breakup be?

How much did they spend on that wedding? What a waste of money!

As you might have guessed, my "parents" nightmare marriage left me commitment-phobic. According to Dr W. Hugh Missildine, "The childhood of persons who suffered from neglect usually reveals a Father who somehow wasn't a Father and a Mother who somehow wasn't a Mother. Thus, in adult life, the neglected 'child of the past' maintains the security of this familiar emptiness …"

He goes on to say, "The relationships of persons who suffered from neglect in childhood resemble those of an actor to his audience. In childhood such a person may have discovered that he could win … momentary attention and love, through his achievements … In such circumstances, a child learns to expect nothing but applause. More than momentary warmth and love do not exist … Closeness threatens the security of neglect on which his 'child of the past' has been nourished. To such a person, closeness is frightening, binding and entrapping …"

Even with beautiful animals that I love and adore, I'm too scared to have one of my own. Though an animal would bring so much love to my life, I think of all the complications. What would I do if I have to travel overseas? What happens if I have to go away for work? I know that there are solutions, but I still feel hesitant.

JOURNAL ENTRY 58 – VICTIM BLAMING

When I've told some people my horror story of abuse, I would sometimes get victim-blaming statements like, "Why didn't you run away?" Or "Maybe if you'd had a different personality it wouldn't have happened." Or, "You fell for it."

What did people expect me to do when I was in kindy and the early years of primary school? Did they expect me to turn into Arnold Schwarzenegger? I repeatedly said "NO" and I still was violated. I would try to run away to my room and I still was violated.

In *The Trials of Gabriel Fernandez*, a six-part crime documentary that premiered on Netflix in 2020, the lawyer, a wise, intelligent man, said something along the lines of, "When people ask why he didn't run away they just don't get it. When you're that age, you can't do anything. Everybody is so much bigger than you and you're so small and you feel so belittled and so bullied."

During my days educating preschool children we would all draw portraits of our family as an art activity and for developing fine motor skills. I observed something poignant about all my children's drawings. They all drew their caregivers in a big size, and they drew themselves in a much smaller size, symbolic of how a child's mind and body are still developing, and therefore children are easily over-powered by an abusive adult. These portraits answer all the ludicrous victim-blaming "why's?"

Always remember that you did the best you could as a child.

JOURNAL ENTRY 59 – ARRESTED DEVELOPMENT

Childhood trauma makes it challenging to transition from a girl into a woman. Our childhoods are a big chunk of our life. It was never going to be water under the bridge. You feel overwhelmed as a grown woman when you're still craving to be loved like a little girl: the title of "Woman" felt too big a burden to bear. Maybe that's why when I laugh, everybody says I sound like I have this cute laugh that makes me sound like an exuberant little girl.

Facing womanhood and feeling forced to wave goodbye to a traumatic childhood while still starving for love and lost for direction is difficult, to say the least. It's like being dumped in the middle of the forest, without a map, compass or emergency kit. I felt like a lost little girl, a "Babe in the Woods."

Think of all the times in your life where you've had to say goodbye or let go before you were ready to. It's really hard, isn't it? It's like grieving. I still want that childhood, the one that was stolen from me.

As a survivor of childhood abuse and childhood sexual abuse, it's important to allow time and space, to grieve for the childhood we didn't receive and to re-parent ourselves.

Maybe being a woman-child isn't so bad. What I've always loved about Marilyn Monroe was her unique ability to balance the sensuality of a woman and the innocence of a girl.

One side of that little girl inside of me longs to be taken care of. Yet, another side of me doesn't want others to see the worst parts of me, like the times I've fallen seriously ill as an adult and have been violently vomiting non-stop.

While lying on the bathroom floor unable to move, I cherished living alone, thankful that during this time no other adult or animal had to see the worst parts of me.

When I went back to work after being so ill, I proudly announced to all my colleagues that I was grateful I'm the only person at work single and living alone, that no significant other was subjected to seeing all of the gross stuff while I was at home vomiting.

One of my male colleagues looked at me puzzled. He said, "When you're with someone, they're supposed to look after you when you're sick. They're supposed to take care of you."

His words struck me, and I thought long and hard about what he'd said to me. Why didn't I want anybody to see me at my worst? Because I didn't trust anybody to care, as nobody cared for me as a child.

In one of the foster homes I stayed in, the mother screamed at me when I vomited. Uneasy from her bitter energy, I felt homesick for the home I've never had.

She was constantly screaming at me and hitting me. One time, she started hitting me and yelling, "You don't deserve to sit at this table and eat with us!" She pushed me off the seat and onto the floor. I felt so scared and stressed I couldn't keep my breakfast down. I threw up the Weet-Bix on the tiled floor.

"Gypsy, you're disgusting!" she screamed, dehumanising me.

She then grabbed me and yelled, "Eat it! Eat your vomit off the floor!" I was horrified at what she was telling me to do, terrified that if I did so I would die. As an adult, feeling I have to vomit is traumatizing. I feel like I'm going to lose my life.

I had many horrifying incidents in foster care throughout my childhood.

Definition of "Forgotten Australian" (a contested term applied by some to the estimated 500,000 children and child migrants who experienced care in institutions or outside a home setting in Australia during the 20th century):

"Children in institutions were sometimes placed in foster homes for short periods, weekends or during holiday periods. Many of these children suffered from neglect and were abused physically, emotionally, or sexually while in care. Survivors to this day still suffer the effects of child abuse. The trauma experienced in care has affected care leavers negatively throughout their adult lives. Their partners and children have also felt the impact, which can then flow through to future generations."[xxxvi]

JOURNAL ENTRY 60 – PRECOGNITIVE DREAMS

Many of my dreams have been precognitive, foretelling a future event.

Once, I dreamt of a girl screaming and crying in the elevator. When I woke up, I wondered whether it was me or someone else. I decided it best to avoid catching the lift that day and I took the stairwell.

When I walked through the foyer later that evening, I heard screaming and crying, "Help!"

I rushed to the elevator door and yelled out, "It's okay, I'll get you out of there. I'll call for help." I phoned the fire brigade and let them know, then I went to the noticeboard next to the letterboxes where the emergency contacts were listed. I called the building manager and other reporting parties. Everybody arrived to help, and we got her out of the elevator safe and well.

Five years before the coronavirus hit, I had this dream. I was in a big room filled with computers and people. All the computers were lit up with a map of Australia coloured in red. Everybody was running around the room.

"Why is our country on red alert?" I asked.

One man said, "We don't know yet, but something is trying to infiltrate Australia. It's an invisible threat."

I left the room and went outside. As I was walking through empty streets, a voice-over in the dream said, "It's safe for everyone to go outside again but be careful." Eventually other people started to come outside and walk on the streets.

I woke up feeling concerned for our country and told everyone about my dream. I wondered if our country would go to war. But in the dream the threat was invisible. Maybe that meant there will be a bomb threat.

Either way, the dream seemed to end on a positive note. Australia handled it. Five years later, the coronavirus hit, and I was constantly seeing maps of Australia in red. The invisible threat in my precognitive dream was COVID-19.

Our minds are powerful. We have an inner intelligence that has the power to sense something from a distance. There is a higher power in this world and it's inside all of us. A higher power that is like the electricity that energises the entire universe.

JOURNAL ENTRY 61 – HEALING IS A PRACTICE

When I became an adult, I decided to report the childhood abuse I had suffered. Remembering the abuse from a male police officer when I reported domestic abuse, I decided to see a female police officer. Though scared, I plucked up the courage to do so.

I gave the police officer details about myself, including the fact that I was studying counselling.

"We rise by lifting others."

~ Robert Ingersoll

"Oh, I think you need to heal yourself before you try to heal others," she said along with other snide comments. I was devastated. That I had monster parents who were the abusers that needed to heal, wasn't even acknowledged by her.

I stood up and walked out, thinking, *Wow, I think I've been through enough. I don't need her speaking to me like I'm damaged goods. She took an oath to show a duty of care towards others. She should know better and not be making inappropriate comments to an extremely high-risk vulnerable human, who has survived childhood abuse.*

I wonder if my mother and stepfather would be thrilled to know I had been rebuffed while trying to reach out for help.

I've coined the term "Survivor Mentality." It refers to using survival stories to help heal others. This is the opposite of the often-heard "Victim Mentality," which refers to people who choose to use their hurt to lash out and hurt others.

After my experience with that victim-blaming police officer, I decided to no longer pursue reporting the crime committed by my parents. I don't want to be on trial. I went through enough stress in my childhood.

I'm also worried people won't believe me. People didn't believe me when I shared my suffering with friends at school. When I told my sister about some of what was going on in the house, she made up excuses for Quirky.

Instead, I wrote this journal about how I survived childhood abuse.

Hearing other's survival stories has helped also to save my life in many ways. For one, I know I'm not alone.

Healing is a practice, a habit one must adapt, just like brushing your teeth and having a shower. To be "fixed" for life, healing has to be a daily practice.

Perhaps for survivors of childhood abuse, it's more about recovering rather than healing.

JOURNAL ENTRY 62 – SURVIVING DOMESTIC VIOLENCE

Given that I had a nasty, cruel stepfather and brother-in-law and survived child abuse, it's no wonder I became a survivor of domestic violence. I had met a man who, though nice to other people, was nasty to me behind closed doors. Eventually, he physically assaulted me, and the police got involved.

One of the male police officers said, "I hope you have better taste in men next time." This comment was not only nasty but ignorant, lacking understanding about domestic abuse.

Partner choice has nothing to do with taste. I didn't have the blueprint from childhood on how to recognise or attract a good man. When I saw that he was nice and charming to other people, I thought that was a sign that he treats people well. Unfortunately, that was just the narcissistic mask he wore in public. In private, the mask dropped, and he was horrible to me.

The police officer should have been congratulating me for leaving. Instead, he was abusive and victim-blaming, talking down to me and violating his vow to show a duty of care. That made him as much an abuser as the man I reported and subsequently left! I hope that the police force will have better taste in men next time.

His misunderstanding was like telling a beached whale to have better taste in locations next time. Just like the whale, my captors had robbed me of the ability to navigate. I had to learn things the hard way because I never had any family to provide me with a foundation.

Not only did I not have a loving family to turn to, or a loving, caring boyfriend when I felt in danger, I couldn't rely on the police force to take me seriously and keep me safe.

The song "Candle in the Wind" has always resonated with me, summing up my childhood of never having anyone to turn to. When you're happy, you enjoy the music and when you're sad you understand the lyrics.

When I told my story to a friend, she said, "Oh, maybe he said that horrible victim-blaming comment to you because he'd just seen a terrible car crash."

"Circumstances do not make a man, they reveal him."

~ Epictetus

Well, if that's the case then the terrible car crash revealed him for being a pig of a man towards a vulnerable high-risk woman. Because whenever I see a terrible car crash, I become MORE LOVING, MORE COMPASSIONATE AND MORE SUPPORTIVE TOWARDS VULNERABLE PEOPLE. I don't be a pig toward them! I don't drive them toward suicide!

For fellow survivors, if you do start dating again, don't kick yourself for "attracting" another abuser/narcissist. As they prefer empaths, they don't want selfish people like themselves. Narcissists try to suck us in and keep us hooked.

JOURNAL ENTRY 63 – OUR HIGHEST SELF

"The butterfly does not look back at the caterpillar in shame, just as you should not look back at your past in shame. Your past was part of your own transformation."

~ Anthony Gucciardi[xxxvii]

We can recover through love along with the joy of giving. We rise above our pain and heal ourselves through lifting others.

Discovering the meaningful, caring world of Early Childhood Education, Counselling and Psychology filled me with joy and purpose because it meant I could give the love and compassion I have within me.

Having a survivor mentality rather than a victim mentality is how we take back our power.

"Change the way you look at things and the things you look at change."

~ Wayne Dyer

Rather than seeing myself as an unloved and unwanted daughter, I now see myself as the woman who cared despite not being cared for in my own childhood. For all the times I supported children through tantrums, suffering, and homesickness. For all the times I wiped their snotty noses, held their hand when they were scared, hugged them to let them know I was happy to see them. For providing them with what I never had: safety, security, and a sense of belonging.

I transformed my greatest pains to become my greatest strengths. That is my legacy.

It is important to remember these facts about survivors:[xxxviii]

- Survivors are strong because they have got through something awful.

- Survivors can be whole again because there are people who care.

- Survivors have stamina and determination because they have made it this far.

- Survivors are courageous because they are raising their voices against abusers.

- Survivors are compassionate because they know the importance of being loving.

- Survivors can make a difference to the world because they have willpower and strength.

Reading many books about Marilyn Monroe was cathartic for me. She's my hero as she was a woman who brought so much joy, beauty and colour to this world, despite the hell she endured as a child.

"God Bless the woman who just wants to do better, be better, feel better; who refuses to give up despite the hell she experiences here on earth."

~ Anonymous

JOURNAL ENTRY 64 – MY BABY CAT

Dear Michael, my baby cat,

While writing this journal to re-parent me, the floodgate of tears opened over losing you. I fear my tears won't stop. Yet I know this pain comes from experiencing something so special with you.

I've always described myself as an unloved and unwanted daughter until you came into my life. You gave me love and you gave me a family. They say family is everything. You were my everything.

I never felt admiration for my mother and stepfather, just repulsion. When I held you in my arms since you were a kitten, I was in awe of your purity and innocence and loving presence. Your purring was like a lullaby to me.

I was in awe of your beauty, your midnight blue–coloured fur. You always looked so romantic.

I cuddled and cradled you every day. We slept in the same bed, both babies growing up together. We were in our world of love together.

After I turned Sweet Sixteen, my Mother became even worse to me and I lost hope, terrified of the long, rough road that lay ahead of me. I felt so unstable and knew this wasn't going to change anytime soon.

Having never been taught how to swim as a child, both figuratively and literally, I was struggling to keep my head above water. Every time I reached out for the lifeboat, my mother kept kicking my hand away. I felt like I was in a deep, dark hole. I knew I wanted a way out, but I just didn't know-how.

Even though you were my life raft, I loved and adored you too much for you to have to be around all of that. How was I ever going to give you the attention you deserved while I was trying to get out of that rut?

Grief is a moving river and I have felt all the ebbs and flows of the loss of you. I can't stop sobbing. I know I have to be patient and accept this grief. I didn't really face and grieve the loss of you properly until I started writing now about my feelings for you. Back then I was still barely in survival mode, I didn't really cry, I was just in a depression.

There are so many shades, depths and layers to the grief. Grief from losing you. Grief because I didn't want to lose you. Grief from not wanting to have disappointed you in any way.

Now that I am re-parenting my inner child, I've allowed myself the time and space to cry over you. I've allowed myself to feel all the feelings I had for you and I will forever hold you close to my heart.

What brings me comfort is to imagine that an angel is cradling you in her arms in heaven, until we meet again.

"There is no death, only a change of worlds."

~ Chief Seattle

I wish I could hold you in my arms again and remind you how special you were to me. I hope you know how much I loved you but that I was just a lost little girl.

Love you always my baby cat.

Love, Gypsy.

•

Dr Robert Neimeyer, Professor of Psychology at the University of Memphis, Tennessee, and author of *Techniques of Grief*

Therapy: Creative Practices for Counseling the Bereaved says that grief is more than simply a series of emotional stages, and healing isn't just about letting time pass.

"Time heals remarkably few wounds of grief because it's not what time does for the bereaved person; it's much more a question of what the bereaved person does with that time that matters." In other words, if we can make sense of our grief, we find meaning and healing in loss—even if we "just" lost a cat.

"Our work," Neimeyer continues, "is all about understanding grieving as a process of trying to reconstruct a world of meaning that has been challenged by loss." He writes that we have to ask ourselves "... what happened, and why and what are its implications for our lives, while also looking at the life we shared with our loved one and carrying it forward in ways we can in their physical absence."

This is why I want to start a foundation in your memory, my beautiful baby cat, called "Family Is Everything" —it's my way of honouring you and honouring what you gave me. Thinking of your absence as only temporary until we meet again comforts me. I love you so much and I hope you feel my love and gratitude for you.

Remember, survivors: when you suffer, hold the things you love close. Don't avoid what brings you joy. You are worthy of love and joy! You are good enough! You deserve happiness!

"Don't let anyone ever make you feel like you don't deserve what you want."

~ Heath Ledger

JOURNAL ENTRY 65 – REPRESSED MEMORY, RESURFACED

After years of being single, I started dating Saba. On the fourth date, I asked his intentions: did he want to exclusively date or not.

"It's important," I said, "that we both know what our expectations are of each other, so neither of us gets hurt."

"No, I don't want to date others and I'm not dating others," he said. "Plus, I don't want you to date others either."

I told him that I wasn't seeing other people.

He added, "And I'm not a two-timer."

After two months of dating, I found out that he was already in a two-year relationship with another girl. I was devastated but glad that I never slept with him even though he pushed for it. I had insisted on taking it slow, which he didn't like. Typical narcissist, they just want to enmesh you as quickly as possible.

It wasn't so much that he was seeing someone else. It was that he lied about it. He told me his mother had been admitted to hospital a few days before, yet it was his girlfriend who was the one in hospital.

I felt betrayed. He disrespected me with his dishonesty. He took away my power to decide if I wanted to be in that kind of situation or not and that made me feel helpless.

His betrayal triggered the traumatic memory of when I felt most betrayed: when my stepfather orally raped me.

Suddenly, I was having flashbacks of his head between my legs when I was a defenceless child.

Noises or smells trigger often repressed memories. For me, the trigger was betrayal, betrayal by a lying and cheating man. I felt preyed upon by men.

I was living alone, and all the flashbacks were flooding back to me as I relived the trauma all over again of being orally raped as a child by my stepfather—transported back in time to feeling like a helpless and powerless child again. It was hell all over again.

I paced the room, feeling as if I was drowning. How did I manage to block this memory out of my mind for decades? I had remembered all the other memories of child sexual abuse. Why not the worst? Blocking out memories, psychologists tell us, protect the victim from being overwhelmed by the trauma.

I remembered pleading with my mum to protect me and she didn't. It made the oral rape even more traumatic as my mother gloatingly watched instead of protecting me. She used me as a Sexual Sacrifice. I feel like throwing up just having to write about this. How could she do that to a child? In many cases, childhood abuse is perpetrated behind the mother's back. Yet, in my survival story, I was betrayed by my very own mother.

This memory was hurting me like hell. She was there. She was a witness, a bystander. My backache. I know what this means. I feel profoundly unsupported. I'm not just imagining this. I know my stepfather did this to me and she knows too.

I ran to the phone and called her.

"How could you do that to me? How could you let that happen to me? How could you let him?" I wailed.

"What are you talking about?"

"YOU LET HIM ORALLY RAPE ME!" I yelled through sobs. I was collapsed on the floor, shaking while clutching the phone.

Silence on the other end of the phone. That silence was my answer. She was taking time to think of her lies.

"No, no! He never did that. I wouldn't let him do that."

"YOU LYING PIG," I yelled, barely able to get the words out, with my body convulsing in an ocean of tears.

Changing tactics, she screamed, "YOU AGREED TO IT. YOU AGREED TO WHAT WAS DONE TO YOU!"

Repulsed, I screamed back. "How dare you blame me for what he did to me! I said 'NO!' I kept saying No, No, No! You kept screaming at me to say, 'Yes!' You were angry at me for repeating No! He screamed at me to do what I was told. You blocked the doorway when I tried to get away and then he overpowered me. You both ganged up on me!"

I dropped the phone and escaped the room. I collapsed in shock on the couch and cried and cried and cried. My back was in excruciating pain. My back is aching just writing about this. I believe in a mind-body connection, and Louise Hay says that back pain represents feeling unsupported in life.

The next morning, the phone was still hanging off the hook. I had confronted her, but I wasn't feeling any better. I was in shock at all the times I had tried so hard to have a mother-daughter relationship with her. Despite my childhood, I've always had strong family values.

Perhaps I had Stockholm Syndrome too, where hostages develop a psychological alliance with their captors during captivity. Emotional bonds may be formed, between captors and captives, during intimate time together, but these are generally considered irrational in light of the danger or risk endured by the victims.[xxxix]

I decided to cut off contact with her for my own welfare and wellbeing. You can forgive someone without letting them and their toxicity back into your life ever again.

Info Point: The No-contact rule. Experts recommend that recovering from narcissistic abuse involves using this strategy.

JOURNAL ENTRY 66 – SELF-ACTUALISATION

One of the greatest gifts a parent can give their child is self-actualisation.

I wanted to be a professional dancer in *Burn the Floor*. But, typical of narcissistic neglectful parents, my "caregivers" refused to give me even one dancing lesson per week.

Eventually, I did a short course on how to teach young children the basic routines in dancing. Even though I was never a professional dancer in *Burn the Floor*, I still found a way to work in the wonderful world of art. Plus, teaching children was such a joy!

Are you able to recall a time or multiple times that you asked for your parent's support to participate in your passions? Did they say Yes or No to you?

Children intrinsically know what they love to do. That's why when I hear someone say, "I don't know what to do with my life. I don't know what job or degree I want to do," I always ask, "Was your self-actualisation repressed as a child by your parents? What did you ask your parents for as a child?"

I also ask, "What did you love doing when you were a child?" Suddenly they are flowing with answers to the question.

So, if you are one of these people who "aren't sure" what you want to do as an adult, then here's my question to you:

What did you love doing as a child? What you loved during childhood will stay on your mind and in your heart forever! My passion for being a writer and artist was within me since I was a child. Your treasure was always within you all along!

When I'm working with children, I always ask, "Tell me about your drawing?" instead of "What did you draw?" With children, it's about the process rather than the product. When I listen to their words, I can hear what they love.

Exercise: Write down your answers as they flow out in response to the question, "What did you love as a child?" When you review your answers, be open-minded about solutions. For example, if you wrote down a football star but you feel it's ludicrous, then remember that there are other ways. You could do a degree in Physical Education or a course in Personal Training. There's always plenty of options in achieving in areas that you love.

Give yourself the gift of self-actualisation. This is one of the best ways to re-parent yourself.

Caregiver Tip: Give your child a choice of hobby/creative outlet and encourage him/her with it. Children need constant encouragement.

JOURNAL ENTRY 67 – PHILOGYNIST

"Men are respectable only as they respect."

~ Ralph Waldo Emerson

Phil was my best friend and like the big brother I never had. He was a journalist, and he was just like one of the Knights of the Round Table.

The word "philogynist," which means a person who likes or admires women, always reminds me of him as he always treated women with respect. That was his legacy! They say a legacy is not something you leave for people but something you leave *in* people. Given that violence against women is an epidemic in Australia and many other countries make his legacy particularly special.

Once he told me that he wished he could travel back in time and carry me away from all the child abuse, just like in the movie, *The Butterfly Effect*. He was a caring friend and brother who always spoke so highly of his two sisters, Emily and Katie.

Phil believed in me and that's one of the greatest gifts you can give someone. He knew that I had studied acting and he encouraged me to audition for an agent. To gain confidence, I took baby steps and found a small agency to audition for. I did the headshots in my blue dress and performed a monologue for Paul Bland, the head booking agent there, while he smoked his cigarette.

The following week, I attended the meeting held for all the new talent within the agency. In front of everyone, my new agent Paul pointed me out and gave me one of the best compliments I've ever received. "Gypsy, when I saw your headshots in that blue dress I thought, *This girl has something to offer*, and you confirmed it when you performed your monologue for me."

Glowing with gratitude, I smiled back at him. In that moment he challenged my self-perception in such a powerful and positive way. While I had always been made to feel like I was nothing but a burden, a shift occurred when I looked into my new agent's eyes and I saw myself as someone who had something to offer. I felt like he had thrown me a lifeline with one simple sentence.

I shared this with Phil who was so happy for me! Genuinely happy for me! They say Australia has the worst Tall Poppy Syndrome, so sometimes not everyone will be happy for you. That's what made Phil so special. He was happy for people when they shared great news. I said to Phil, "I know Paul swings the other way which is why I thought he wouldn't even notice me and yet he made me feel so seen!"

"Then you know that he's not trying to get into your pants," Phil said. "You know that he meant those kind words."

Paul helped secure so many paid gigs for me in films, television and commercials plus some fun events too! In one of those events, I dressed up in a Marilyn Monroe dress with a Bridgette Bardot hairstyle, and had my photo taken on the red carpet!

I reminded Phil that this positive experience happened because he had believed in me—A man who wanted to see a woman shine like a star! I always told him how grateful I was for his friendship.

Before Phil passed over, he made a mixed tape of songs for me that I will always hold close to my heart. It's bizarre how we go into denial at first when we are faced with devastation. I remember the female nurses ushered me into a tiny room at the hospital, away from the public waiting area. One of the nurses looked at me and announced three words: "He didn't survive."

I immediately yelled, "NO! I DON'T BELIEVE YOU! Where is he? YOU HAVE TO LET ME SEE HIM!" When they took me to him, I truly believed that I would find signs of life. I rushed over to him lying on the bed, his face looked so blue. I checked his pulse, I checked for a heart rate, but I couldn't feel anything. I held his hand and it was cold, so cold.

One of the hardest things about someone passing over is that life still goes on for the rest of us. When I was walking through the grocery store like a depressed zombie, I watched everyone else go about their life. I remember wanting everyone and everything to just stop even for just a moment. I remember wishing I could ask everyone to please stop and have a minute of silence. I remember desperately wanting so much to hold space for a man who had been a very dear friend to me, a very special man who had treated me like his little sister and had given me a sense of family.

One of the songs he chose for me as his musical gift to me was, "Ohh Child" by the Five Stairsteps.

"Look for the helpers. You will always find people who are helping."

~ Fred Rogers

JOURNAL ENTRY 68 – CHRIS, A COMPASSIONATE WITNESS

"Some days I am everything that I hate. There's nothing if the truth won't survive. That I can create, that I can write, that I can express, that is the light at the end of the tunnel. That is how you win the battle."

~ Michael Hutchence

I was in Melbourne on a work trip and had experienced one too many dramas while down there. In my friend Chris's kitchen, I had a nervous breakdown and broke down into sobs.

I blurted out some of the trauma from my childhood. I was so upset about my current situation that part of my childhood regurgitated out of me.

"When I was a little girl, my stepfather used to sexualise my mother in front of me," I told him through sobs.

I realised I had said this out loud when I saw the look of anger and repulsion on his face.

In a raised voice he said, "Well, he was f—— in the head!"

"I know. I know he was," I said.

"I don't want to say anything about your mother."

"I understand," I said as I wiped away my tears.

"He had no respect for your mother to do that to her in front of you," he added.

Sobbing, I told him, "All my life I've wanted to be successful, and today I realised that not only am I not successful but that I'm not even a good survivor."

 "This is what movies are made about," he said. "You are a survivor. You're a resilient survivor."

The next day I took a flight back to Sydney. While at the airport waiting for my flight, I grabbed a coffee, sat down and rummaged through my bag to find my earphones.

My phone beeped. There was a message from Chris. "You are a Resilient Survivor."

Grateful for his words, I could feel myself getting teary again. I turned on the music to distract myself. I reflected upon the message of the movie *Rocky* that had always inspired me. "Now, if you know what you're worth, then go out and get what you're worth. But you gotta be willing to take the hits, and not pointing fingers saying you ain't where you wanna be because of him, or her, or anybody. Cowards do that and that ain't you. You're better than that!"

"Think like a Queen. A Queen is not afraid to fail. Failure is another stepping stone to greatness."

~ Oprah Winfrey

JOURNAL ENTRY 69 – A VIEW FROM THE TOP

"The roughest road often leads to the top."

~ Unknown

I was so excited when I found out two of my favourite American authors were doing a speaking tour in Sydney, Australia. I had to go!

After the seminar, Dr Wayne Dyer and Louise Hay both announced they would spend a short time in the foyer signing books. I was thrilled, as I had brought their books from home with me, hoping to have them signed.

Louise Lynn Hay was an American motivational author and the founder of Hay House. She authored several New Thought self-help books, including the 1984 book, *You Can Heal Your Life.*

Wayne Walter Dyer was an American self-help author and motivational speaker. His first book, *Your Erroneous Zones* (1976), is one of the bestselling books of all time, with an estimated 100 million copies sold to date.

By the time I managed to make it out of the convention centre stadium, Wayne and Louise were already surrounded by at least a few hundred people wanting signatures.

So, I went away, had a coffee and something to eat, bought some more of both their books on sale at the stand, and then returned.

They were both gone. Everyone was gone. How? I only walked away for 15 minutes.

My inner child was crying. *Everybody always leaves. I'm always abandoned. I'm always left behind. Everybody else got their signatures and I didn't get my wants and needs met. I'm always forgotten; I'm always left out; I'm always excluded.*

A lady was packing away some other tables. I've always been persistent and so I asked, "Where are Louise Hay and Wayne Dyer? I bought their books to get their signatures. Where did they go?"

"Everyone's gone. Wayne and Louise ran out of time for signatures."

Nobody ever has time for me, my inner child cried silently to myself.

I wanted to burst into tears. Suddenly, I heard another voice from up high above.

"You can come up here with me, if you like."

I turned around and looked up. Standing at the top of the stairs in front of the doorway to the green room was the very man himself, Dr Wayne Dyer.

"I'll sign your books in the green room," he added as I looked up at him in awe.

My inner child went from crying to squealing with excitement at his invitation. I was going to get my signature; and in the greenroom too!

For an aspiring author like me, it was an incredible invitation to receive an exclusive signing in the green room!

I followed him up the stairs with all of his books and cassette tapes in hand.

My inner child's voice was racing with pure joy. *He's making time for me! He was about to go on his break to the green room and drink, eat and relax. He's invited me up here to do more signatures, even though he didn't have to be bothered with anybody anymore. He's not treating me like a drag, chore or burden like Mum and Quirky did. He's happy to be kind to me!*

I was gushing. "You have no idea how much this means to me. Thank you so much for this!"

I placed all of his books and cassettes on the table and smiled with gratitude. I glowed as I watched him sign them all.

"It was incredible watching you up on stage speaking."

He put the pen down and said, "Thank you," in that wonderful American accent of his and gave me a warm fatherly hug. I was always fascinated with America and here I was with an American author!

Then another magical moment happened.

But first I will digress. When someone is so loving and so positive, they are operating at a high energy frequency. That magical moment when he put the pen down and hugged me, I could feel family love resonating out of him. I could literally *feel* his loving energy. In all of my childhood, I'd never felt that until I was in his arms.

He then walked over to the kitchen area.

As I bundled all he signed for me and put them in my bag, he asked, "Would you like a cupcake?"

There was a platter of beautiful cupcakes reserved for the speakers/authors at the seminar.

Amazed but too shy to accept, I said, "Oh, I already ate but thank you."

"Well how about saving one for later? That's what I always say to my children." He put a paper towel over one of the cupcakes, wrapped it up and handed it to me.

My mum never made me lunch, she only made Quirky's lunch. Yet, here was someone else's father insisting on giving me a cupcake. I felt so special, so seen and valued. My feelings mattered as did the simple human need for nourishment.

"Oh, thank you. That's very sweet. Please come back to Australia," I said as I walked toward the door, flying inside.

"I will."

I will be forever grateful for my own awe-inspiring moments with him. How magical, what a wonderful crescendo after a special seminar. This was a memory I'll treasure forever.

JOURNAL ENTRY 70 – GREAT THINGS CAN COME OF GREAT PAIN

"How people treat you is their karma; how you react is yours."

~ Wayne Dyer

As I walked home after the seminar, I was on a high from feeling the fatherly love that resonated from his hug. I want to feel like this forever! He emanated such pure loving energy.

I felt like he had given me a cup of water and I felt recovered and recharged to run my race again.

I could feel my dreams rekindling inside me again. Maybe I could start dancing again. Maybe I could start writing again. Maybe I could pursue a dream and maybe it could come true.

I ran back home in childlike excitement.

When I arrived home, I took the cupcake out of my handbag to unwrap it. I decided it was too special to eat. I put it in a container in the fridge so I could continue to admire it for days. After being dehumanised for such a long time as a child, I wanted to savour that cupcake and make that moment last.

It wasn't about the cupcake. It was what the cupcake represented. If you are deprived of your basic needs as a child, like love and food, it can make you feel hopeless. Yet, hope is what all fathers are supposed to give their children. My stepfather always used to yell at me, "Don't get your hopes up." When Wayne Dyer gave me that cupcake, he gave me hope that felt like the future will be better than the past.

Symbolic of a "pass on the torch" moment, that meant maybe one day I'll turn from aspiring author to published author, just like him!

A wonderful and loving person who used his past to help other people! I was always so inspired by his story that he had been fatherless too and in and out of foster homes. I saw so much of myself in him.

I know that Great Things can come from Great Pain. His taking the time to give me that personalised book signing was something great. It was all LOVE!

"Not all great things come from great pain. Sometimes it's love. Not everything's a sacrifice."

~ Darius, *Atlanta* series

Just like I wrote this journal out of love.

Years later, he became a minister to officiate the marriage between Ellen DeGeneres and Portia de Rossi. He was a man who had worn many different caps and brought joy to many different people's lives.

JOURNAL ENTRY 71 – TAPASYA

"Tapasya includes control over one's physical body, speech, thoughts and mind. It helps an individual meditate properly, control the ego, and create a disciplined mind that will not accept the desires of the body."

~ Yogapedia

Tapasya is about taking responsibility for your life. It includes many forms.

For example, facing life head-on with no drugs, no cigarettes and no alcohol.

Doing yoga because yoga requires discipline, self-control and denial of bodily desires.

Being a vegan and practicing pure non-violence toward all living beings.

Eliminating anger and destructive impulses to avoid hurting others.

Tapasya is also about your resolve, about being disciplined with your dreams and goals regarding career, relationships and life in general. That means you must overcome obstacles and never give up.

A burning desire must fuel your discipline. They say the strongest steel goes through the hottest fire and that diamonds are made under pressure.

As I write this, I can still hear the fatherly voice of Dr Wayne Dyer and still feel his loving presence.

"With everything that has happened to you, you can either feel sorry for yourself or treat what has happened as a gift. Everything is either an opportunity to grow or an obstacle to keep you from growing. You get to choose."

~ Wayne Dyer

As a lover of literature, I have read many classics, from Wayne Dyer's books to *Pride and Prejudice*, to *King Arthur and Camelot*, *Wuthering Heights*, *Sense and Sensibility* and *Lolita*!

I love to sit outside in my garden and enjoy the sunshine while I read.

Out of all the classics I've read, *Lolita* perhaps resonates with me especially and always will.

"What I heard was but the melody of children at play ... and then I knew that the hopelessly poignant thing was not Lolita's absence from my side, but the absence of her voice from that concord."

~ Vladimir Nabokov, *Lolita*

"As a case history, *Lolita* will become, no doubt, a classic in psychiatric circles," writes John Ray, Jr., Ph.D. "As a work of art, it transcends its expiatory aspects; and still more important to us ... is the ethical impact the book should have on the serious reader; for in this poignant personal study there lurks a general lesson; the wayward child, the egotistic mother, the panting maniac—these are not only vivid characters in a unique story: they warn us of dangerous trends; they point out potent evils."

After I put the book down, I admired what a beautiful morning it was in my garden, with the neighbour's beautiful cat keeping me company.

"I reflected upon the lesson of Lolita *... 'Lolita should make all of us, parents, social workers, educators—apply ourselves with still greater vigilance and vision to the task of bringing up a better generation in a safer world.'"*

~ John Ray, Jr., Ph.D.

After a childhood of being locked away in a dark room, it is truly heaven to feel the sunshine on my skin, to see the birds flying through the sky, to listen to them chirping from the trees.

I could hear Wayne Dyer's loving and fatherly voice inside my head. "Don't die with your music still inside of you."

Someone once said that a bird sings in the morning to let other birds know that they made it through the night.

Maybe that's why I create art; maybe that's why I wrote this journal.

It's my music to let other survivors of child abuse know that I made it through the darkness.

I hope it gives you the hope that you can make it through the darkness too.

THE BEGINNING!

AFTERWORD

"In the space of letting go, she let it all be …. And the sun and moon shone forevermore …"

~ Ernest Holmes

APPENDIX

i.	mnn.com/lifestyle/arts-culture/stories/what-is-kintsugi
ii.	dcp.wa.gov.au/ChildProtection/ChildAbuseAndNeglect/Pages/Childabuseandneglect.aspx
iii.	pcar.org/learn-examples-of-child-sexual-abuse
iv.	dcp.wa.gov.au/ChildProtection/ChildAbuseAndNeglect/Pages/Childabuseandneglect.aspx
v.	stopitnow.org/ohc-content/clearing-up-common-misunderstandings
vi.	sane.org
vii.	unrighteousdominion.org
viii.	stopitnow.org/advice-column-entry/is-groping-and-dirty-talk-in-front-of-children-okay
ix.	childaustralia.org.au/wp-content/uploads/2017/02/CA-Statement-Pedagogy.pdf
x.	acecqa.gov.au/sites/default/files/acecqa/files/QualityInformationSheets/QualityArea5/QualityArea5OrangeRelationshipsWithChildren.pdf
xi.	acecqa.gov.au/sites/default/files/acecqa/files/QualityInformationSheets/QualityArea5/QualityArea5OrangeRelationshipsWithChildren.pdf
xii.	acecqa.gov.au/sites/default/files/acecqa/files/QualityInformationSheets/QualityArea5/QualityArea5OrangeRelationshipsWithChildren.pdf
xiii.	acecqa.gov.au/sites/default/files/acecqa/files/QualityInformationSheets/QualityArea5/QualityArea5OrangeRelationshipsWithChildren.pdf
xiv.	acecqa.gov.au/sites/default/files/acecqa/files/QualityInformationSheets/QualityArea5/QualityArea5OrangeRelationshipsWithChildren.pdf
xv.	nationaleczema.org/eczema-emotional-wellness/
xvi.	animals.mom.me/dolphins-use-sonar-5591.html
xvii.	thedodo.com/in-the-wild
xviii.	peta.org/wp-content/uploads/2019/06/SeaWorld-Dolphin-White-Paper.pdf
xix.	stopitnow.org/ohc-content/defining-child-sexual-abuse
xx.	stopitnow.org/help-guidance/prevention-tools
xxi.	eige.europa.eu/gender-based-violence/what-is-gender-based-violence
xxii.	stopitnow.org/advice-column-entry/is-groping-and-dirty-talk-in-front-of-children-okay
xxiii.	stopitnow.org/advice-column-entry/is-groping-and-dirty-talk-in-front-of-children-okay
xxiv.	aplaceofhope.com
xxv.	americanhumane.org
xxvi.	stopitnow.org/advice-column-entry/are-these-boyfriends-behaviors-abusive
xxvii.	en.wikipedia.org/wiki/Betrayal_trauma
xxviii.	stopitnow.org
xxix.	stopitnow.org
xxx.	stopitnow.org/ohc-content/clearing-up-common-misunderstandings
xxxi.	1 Corinthians 13:4–7 (NIV)
xxxii.	animals.mom.me/ladybugs-considered-good-luck-5881.html
xxxiii.	ohchr.org/en/professionalinterest/pages/crc.aspx
xxxiv.	goodreads.com/work/quotes/1015554-matilda
xxxv.	foundersguide.com/top-5-benefits-of-learning-chess/
xxxvi.	en.wikipedia.org/wiki/ForgottenAustralians
xxxvii.	facebook.com/AnthonyGucciardi/
xxxviii.	https://napac.org.uk/wp-content/uploads/2016/06/Recovering_from_childhood_abuse.pdf
xxxix.	en.wikipedia.org/wiki/Stockholm_syndrome